GREAT SAND DUNES NATIONAL PARK

BETWEEN LIGHT AND SHADOW

D0506464

PHOTOGRAPHY AND ESSAYS BY JOHN B. WELLER

WESTCLIFFE PUBLISHERS

westcliffepublishers.com

For all the people who work to protect wildlands.

Sunset from the End of Medano Creek

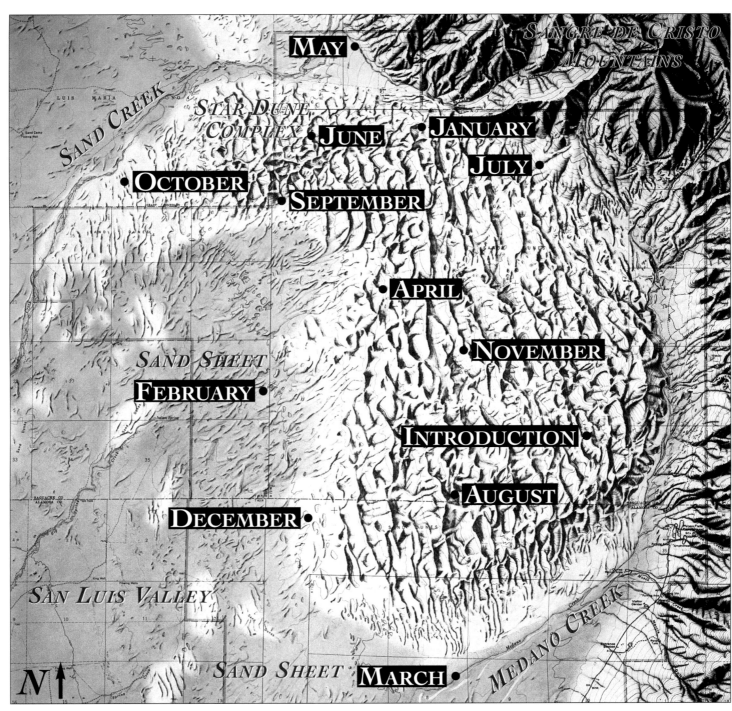

MAY •

SANGRE DE CRISTO
MOUNTAINS

LUIS MARIA

STAR DUNE
COMPLEX

SAND CREEK

JUNE

JANUARY

JULY •

OCTOBER •

SEPTEMBER

APRIL •

SAND SHEET

NOVEMBER

FEBRUARY •

INTRODUCTION •

AUGUST •

DECEMBER •

MEDANO CREEK

SAN LUIS VALLEY

SAND SHEET

MARCH •

N ↑

*MAP COURTESY OF **U.S. GEOLOGICAL SURVEY** • 1 INCH = 1.25 MILES*

TABLE OF CONTENTS

Windswept Dunes #1

Windswept Dunes #2

Sunrise over Frosted Dunes

The sign planted in the sand read: "Entering Great Sand Dunes Wilderness, where man himself is a visitor that does not remain." Kangaroo rat tracks scurried around the signpost, crossing older coyote tracks. Beyond, surreal dunes and white-capped mountains rose into the sky like cardboard cutouts. We stood for a long time just looking up. My stomach did a quick flip-flop and we started to climb.

It was November, and I had come with a friend to watch a meteor shower. We struggled up one of the most difficult routes into the dunes, hauling cameras, tripods, sleeping bags, water, a camp stove, and a meal. We willed ourselves to the top. Every step was pain. But we were rewarded with an isolated camping spot at the bottom of a dune bowl. The air was still, the dune warm. A smooth rim of sand formed the horizon, and the blue sky clamped down over us. We laid out our sleeping bags on the sand and looked up into that blue.

Night descended, settling into the dune bowl, bringing cold air. We cooked our meal and ate quickly, retreating into our sleeping bags. It was already two degrees below zero. Stars poked through the black velvet, and the heavens spun. Suddenly, a streak of light arched silently across the whole sky. Then another, shorter, but bright blue, sliced through the black. The show was on.

Shooting stars slashed at the sky. They left afterimages in my eyes. At the middle of the shower, there were never fewer than four meteors in the sky at any time. A huge blue one—as thick as my index finger held at arm's length—shot halfway across, then exploded into two smaller streaks that sped off in different directions. We both gasped. Hours later I drifted off as best I could in the biting cold, shooting stars still raking the sky.

When I awoke a few hours later, shivering in the predawn, the sky was still full of streaking meteors. I walked to the top of the dune bowl and looked out across the turbulent sea of sand. The dunes were white with frost. I started to photograph, jumping around between shots to warm myself up. Shooting stars disappeared into the brightening horizon. Then the sun rose, flooding the world with light, and the frosted grains of sand sparkled like diamonds. My friend joined me at the top of the ridge and we greeted the brilliant day with frozen bananas and ice water.

As the sun rose higher, the dunes became increasingly bizarre. The only frost left lay in the shadows of snaking ridges. The patches of frost were like mirrors, reflecting sky. It was as if the dunes had been painted with great swaths of electric blue. The patches were so reflective that at one point, I saw a cloud passing in one of them. I couldn't take photographs fast enough. In an hour, all the frost and reflections had disappeared into the still air. The dunes were now warm again, so I took off my boots and sank my feet into the sand. My friend, sitting on top of another dune, had done the same.

The whole place seemed to be a contradiction—a high desert nestled between a backbone of 14,000-foot peaks and some of Colorado's richest wetlands. Local weather can be fierce, with sand temperatures ranging from twenty-eight degrees below zero to more than 140 degrees. Pockets of grassland persevere, surrounded by miles of active dunes. Creeks run over open sand. Some specialized creatures live here and nowhere else in the world. Yet, sitting there in November with my feet covered in warm sand, everything seemed so simple.

My youth had been filled with camping, hiking, and birding. I had studied nature under countless mentors, had been weaned on the outdoors. I had trained in photography and lived in a national park. But now I ran my own nature photography business, struggling for money, drawn in a thousand different directions. My senses were continually assaulted. My daily activities and thoughts were like jumbled sound bites.

Looking out over the dunes, I felt drawn in only one direction: in. I was sitting at the edge of wilderness, a place where people are still just visitors. The dunes are raw, unfiltered by culture. They are unprocessed, unpackaged, unspun. I internalized the value of this, swallowing the concept. I made the decision right there, with my feet in the warm sand. I would walk out into the dunes—to touch them, to absorb their nuance, to see clearly.

Starting the following spring, and for one week nearly every month for the next three years, I took my pack—loaded with up to 115 pounds of cameras, water, food, and camping gear—and walked deep into the dunes. I submitted to their detail.

I spent entire days watching light move across the dunes, circus beetles and giant sand treader camel crickets digging holes in the sand, and hummingbirds drinking nectar from trumpet flowers. I witnessed windstorms whipping dust-devil sand spirits into the air at sixty miles per hour, snowstorms coating the dunes with tumbleweed rafts of snowflakes as the temperature dropped thirty degrees in five minutes, and lightning striking less than a hundred feet away. I met coyotes face to face. I watched the wind stop.

As I look back on my decision, I didn't realize what I was getting myself into. But my body and equipment have adapted. My definitions of discomfort have changed. I now crave the feeling of sand in my hair. I knew I would be different at the end. I didn't know how much I would learn.

With each trip, I became more vividly awake, more aware of each and every step that I took on the dunes, more cognizant of the beauty and interconnectedness of all things. Just underneath the shifting sands I found the reflection of a face, and it was my own. Once seen, the image was impossible to forget, for it illuminated fragility, beauty, and the necessity of peace.

Dune Shapes and Frosted Shadows Reflecting the Sky

Ravens

MAY: GHOST CREEK

The movement was suddenly hypnotic as I walked through the new-green swells of a wet spring's grassland in the late morning. A thousand clustered balls of yellow flowers on two-foot-high stalks swayed asynchronously in the eddying breezes on a low dune-turned-hillside. With the shadowed and muted dunes as a backdrop, the blooms taught a surprising lesson in the appreciation of the color yellow.

At the northern edge of the sand dunes is the Sangre de Cristo Range, and where mountain meets dune, they swirl together. Sandy soil gives way suddenly to scree rock. There is a singular rock outcropping that sits half a mile from any other rock of its size, a tiny offshore island in the lake of moving sand. The rock juts out of the sand like the bow of a buried ship, confronting the dunes and anchoring a vestige of the montane ecosystem: a massive shrub and a miniature juniper tree.

As the waves of sand lap on the shore of mountains, they bury the ecosystem alive, swallowing full-grown pine trees. There is a particular place on the northern side where a thirty-foot-tall wave of sand, pushing its way up the mountain, has killed and half buried a fifty-foot-tall pine tree. The middle branches now form a cage, arching down, the tips buried in the sand. Many times, I have walked up to sit in the cage and try to understand the speed of the changing landscape from the perspective of a tree.

There is a form of riptide that helps confine the lake of sand to its shores. Plants recolonize and anchor the sand, incorporating it into the mountain. They absorb the waves and bury dunes under layers of dead and decaying plant material. The longer the sand is stabilized, the closer it comes to being a soil. The stabilized sand allows for a treasury of plants to flourish that can't live on active dunes. There are places where pine trees are riding out the rough waves of parabolic dunes successfully, as well as places so stable that fifty-foot-tall pine trees have actually regrown on top of the sand.

I stopped for breakfast at the rock outcrop, as I usually do on this side of the dunes. Farther on, at an appropriate spot, I lay down on a soft bed of needles in the cooling shade of a pine and felt the slap of sand on my face with each strong gust of wind. I took a nap with the sound of the wind through the needles, and the rasping and chuckling of Steller's jays.

The cacti were blooming. Prickly pears blossomed lemon yellow and saffron peach, and the white petals of the yuccas' bell-shaped flowers were folded under maroon calyxes, waiting for nightfall to open for the pronuba moth, their only pollinator. Refreshed from my nap, I reshouldered my pack and continued through the savanna until I came to the deep cut of a seasonal creek snaking its way through a procession of vegetated dunes. A swallow swerved overhead as I skidded my way down the forty-foot slope to the bottom of the wash, the steeply angled walls of sand and plants rising to cut off my view. I came to rest on the creekbed of a tributary of Sand Creek, which flows on the northern edge of the dunes. The first thing I noticed was that the insects had changed. A giant blue dragonfly zigzagged past like an alien ship. There were clouds of gnats in the stunted cottonwoods that grew out of the narrow bank, and a few mosquitoes whined insistently.

The mountain was pulling the stream backward, upslope, retracting the long tongues of water. I had descended right at the point where the water from the upstream flood was sinking back into the sand. The creekbed was composed almost entirely of sand, meaning that water levels in the creek would directly depend on the level of the underlying water table. When the water table drops to the point at which the stream will fit nicely underground, and when, shortly thereafter, the flow loses the power to flood over unsaturated sand, the desert swallows the stream whole. The change was more or less even across the width of the channel. Just a couple hundred feet upstream, there was water across the whole of the forty-foot-wide creekbed. A few fingers of water extended toward me, indicating the deeper channels, but where I stood, I was on firm, wet sand.

Facing downstream, the path of the deepest channels continued as wet sand. The rest of the streambed made the transition to dry sand. My eyes wandered along the path of wet sand as it snaked around the corner of a giant bend in the gulch, and I saw a ghost.

New green grasses were matted down against the sand all along the sides of the drying creekbed, signs of a recent shoreline. It was as if I had put on a pair of astral spectacles, for I could now see the ghost of the tumbling creek as it had been only weeks before, at the height of the spring runoff.

In my mind's eye, the ghost creek spilled its eight inches of water across the sand, pooling and eddying around carved sand corners, rocks, and a few woody shrubs that lined the shore. I imagined the unstable feeling of sinking in saturated sand and the chill of ghost water topping the lips of my boots, swamping my socks. I started to walk downstream.

I followed the ghost creek around bend after bend. It snaked back and forth, and I was always within sight of two sharp bends. In between the gentlest bends, I could see a hundred feet in front and a hundred feet behind, before the towering walls of the gulch melded and swept around a corner. The creek swung right, then left, then right again, and on the fourth turn, the walls of the gulch converged and squeezed the thirty-foot-wide creekbed into a six-foot-wide channel.

It was quiet as I entered the narrows. A tiger swallowtail floated through thick alders and willows that were anchored, like the steep sand walls of the canyon, by boulders the size of a man—reminders that this was both mountain and desert. The entrance of the hollow was heavily guarded by vegetation and by a thick log that had wedged itself between two of the boulders.

When I focused I could almost hear the water.

Underneath the disquieting stillness I could imagine the roar of the ghost creek as it accelerated around the corner and was forced through the eye of the needle. Riffraff was plastered against the boulders and held aloft by the willows, recording torrents of waist-high water. Water had jammed plant litter against every barrier —green pine needles, and sticks, and pieces of bark and leaves, and sand caught in all of it. Driftwood had crammed up against rocks, and against other driftwood, and against the shoreline, and against exposed roots of plants. The water had boiled over and around the boulders, stripping the grasses from the lower walls, tearing at the bank. The force of the image almost knocked me over, and I gasped for air as I was swept around another narrow bend and was deposited on soft sand at the widening of the gulch.

The signs of the commotion disappeared as quickly as they had appeared, as the ghost water dispersed across the widened channel, there only a foot deep. A hummingbird zoomed over my head, the whir of wings erupting and instantly receding. Suddenly, the air was perfumed, and there, on my left, was a massive boulder the size of two men. The plastered debris and the sculpted sand revealed that the water had been pushed up against the face of the rock and had been diverted around it, leaving a two-foot section of shoreline basically untouched by the current. Nestled in the protective stream-shadow of the boulder was the source of the perfume. A head-high wild rosebush in brilliant bloom stood humming, full of grace and bees. I counted eighty-four blossoms. Each flower was resplendent perfection. I couldn't move for a long time.

It had become hot. Closer to where Ghost Creek runs into Sand Creek, the vegetation fell back and the walls of the gulch turned back into dunes. I passed through a tall fence, and the creek I had been following was no longer wilderness. Though it flowed the same, it flowed through land that showed signs of use. Ragweed grew on the hillside, probably brought by the same cows that had left the now-dried cow patties in the wash, and I found my first piece of garbage.

The signs of recent water became faint, and finally the evidence of this year's runoff was swallowed by the sand. The ghost creek disappeared more than a quarter of a mile from where it would have converged with the nearly year-round flow of Sand Creek, but the faded signatures of older runoffs continued. Ghost creek's older cousins must have been fearsome.

It had become very hot. The walls of the gulch dropped away. There were deer prints in the soft sand, and as I came around the last bend of the dried creekbed, I was greeted by low, sculpted sandbanks and a wall of cottonwoods, the undersides of green leaves flashing in the wind like fish scales. A few minutes later, I was enjoying their shade. I could now hear the real water of Sand Creek. I sat for a moment in the cool shade as a yellow warbler practiced jazz:

a-siss-siss-sih, bibb-bibb-bih, ðiðð-ðiðð-ðih, ðah.
a-siss-siss-sih, bibb-bibb-bih, ðiðð-ðiðð-ðih, ðah.
a-siss-siss-sih, bibb-bibb-bih, ðiðð-ðiðð-ðih, ðah.

The water glowed a pale green and deep yellow as it tumbled over rocks. Upon seeing, at last, actual deep, cold, rushing water, I dropped my pack, dropped my clothes, and washed off my accumulated load of sand in the waters of Sand Creek.

Predawn Abstract

Sunrise Abstract

Raven Tracks

Raven over the 4th Dimension

Dune Shapes

Backlit Ridges

JUNE: YELLOW EYES

The stag beetle turned around to face me and reared back on its hind legs, head held high, mandibles open. I admit that I had sneaked up on it from behind and had prodded it with a blade of grass. Its scientific name is *Pseudolucanus mazama*, but its common name, "pinching bug," relates a more accurate image. Though harmless, its pincers were ferocious. I did not prod it again. The armor on the beetle's back was pitted with tiny divots like a golf ball. Between every joint and segment, fine golden hairs formed a barrier to the sand. The same golden hairs covered its legs, pointing downward, perhaps to stop it from sinking. I sat still until the beetle backed down and continued on its course traversing a slope, pulling itself across with its front four legs. It used its two back legs purely as skis, cutting a ledge with the downhill back leg to keep its heavy abdomen from sliding.

It had taken two days of hiking to get to my camp, a bowl between interwoven dunes at the northern edge of the dune mass. The sun was already starting to bake, and visible waves of heat rose off the sand. I felt lazy. I stretched out, burrowing my hands down into the cool sand eight inches under the surface. I started to doze off, but suddenly felt painful pinpricks up and down the backsides of my exposed arms, legs, and neck. I jumped up, brushing off my attackers. They were mites. A virtual carpet of the tiny arachnids had emerged from the sand. I no longer felt sleepy.

The almost perfectly camouflaged mites were each the size of about five grains of sand. Their red legs, thinner than hairs, were barely visible even at close range. They cruised across the sand in all directions. I put on protective long pants, despite the heat, and knelt down to watch them. The wind picked up for a moment, and it carried mites along with it. Once dropped, one of the windblown mites tipped itself up perpendicular to the sand and started to dig, pushing stones a fifth the size of its body out of the way as it went. In seconds, it had buried itself completely. The sand bulged, sagged, and then was still. I gave the mite a measured minute, then blew away layers of sand to find it. In that minute, the mite had gone down almost an inch.

The currency of this tiny world is biomass, and I witnessed an exchange. The mites had caught a beetle. The circus beetle was alive but stood stationary as twelve mites clambered around on its head. All the mites on the beetle had a slight green sheen to them. It appeared that the first thing the mites had done was eat the antennae, cutting off the beetle's communication. Without the necessary stimuli, the beetle was as good as immobilized.

Mites seemed to be roaming around the sand more or less at random. But when one happened to come within about an inch of the beetle, it would change directions and join the attack, as if it could smell the food. After twenty minutes, there were more than thirty mites on the beetle, attacking from every angle—the leg joints, the suture along the back, the head, and the abdomen. In an hour and a half, the beetle had fallen on its side, and the mites had broken through the armor in several places. All of the attacking mites had the same green sheen. The beetle was still moving.

Coyote

The long pants that I was wearing were black, and I had become hot and sweaty. I never carry water for anything but drinking, so I scrubbed away the sweat with handfuls of sand. I switched back into shorts, packed my daypack, and walked out into the stiffening wind. By two o'clock, it was a gale. Gritty sand peppered me from head to toe, stinging my legs, arms, and cheeks, bouncing off my ski goggles. My ears rang with the sound. I stopped to refill my water bottle from the water bag hanging off my pack and received a jarring electric shock. The wind had pounded the water bag so hard that it had ionized the water, temporarily turning it into a battery. But by six o'clock, the air was nearly still.

Shadow filled the hollow and outlined the snaking curve of the ridgeline as the last of the wind lifted sand spirits, exhaustedly, into the air. The sun hung in the sky in such a way that the ridge cast its shadow down the whole of one side of the dune. Yet the tips of the few grasses on the shadowed side, which stood six inches above the surface of the smooth slope, were still illuminated. They caught the light and sparkled against the darkened sand.

They passed like apparitions.

Out of the corner of my eye, I glimpsed a distant smooth movement, eloquent speed. My breath stopped in my throat: coyotes. They were heading my way. They cruised across the sand—fast feet, light as feathers, covering more ground in thirty seconds than I could in twenty minutes, even without the weight of my pack. They dropped out of sight behind the mound of a dune, and then they materialized again, on top of the ridge.

The coyotes skimmed over the dune with movements so fluid that their bodies seemed to pulse and ripple. Explosions of sand flew up from their feet, the only evidence that they were touching the ground at all. I fumbled to get my camera out of the pack in time. But before I could manage to get it onto a tripod, the coyotes jumped the snaking ridgeline, and for five seconds they were lit, nearly white, against the dark shadow on the slip face of the dune before they disappeared behind another fold of sand.

They passed like apparitions.
They passed like part of a dusty fable.

And two sets of yellow eyes,
which met my own for a split second,
were like deep pools of reflective water,
defiant and unafraid.

The coyotes disappeared for almost a minute and then reappeared some fifteen hundred feet away. My camera was now securely mounted, and through my longest lens I caught another glimpse of those yellow eyes as the coyotes turned and scrutinized me once more, from almost a third of a mile. I only know the distance because, as I watched, one of them sat down on the top of a low dune and started to howl.

Abstracted Dune Ridge and Sky

Separated from its source by a second and a half,
the sound of howling floated, disembodied, across the dunes,
giving voice to presence.

It streaked along my scalp.
It seemed to come from every shadowed hollow of my mind.
It seemed to be the voice of time.

What their line must have seen:
the endless high prairie and the roar of unthinkable storms.

The waking of human civilizations in the San Luis Valley,
and the first campfire,
flickering orange light against the rich black of uncut land,
under the vastness of a new-moon sky.

Weary explorers, tumbling down mountain passes.
Wars and mines and roads and airplanes overhead.

There seemed to be a note of sadness in the voice.

Even if the eyes,
reflective pools of sunset water,
remained defiant.

With one last glance, the coyotes topped a distant crest and dissolved into the dunes.

Wind

Dunes at Sunrise

Dunes in Rain

The concentrated taste of wild raspberries still stung my tongue as I gingerly raised my finger to my face and gazed into the echoing depths of two enormous, beautifully blue compound eyes. The June beetle clung jealously to my finger, almost disquietingly tight, with the multitudes of hooks on its legs and pincerlike toes. From either side of a wide snout, red antennae blossomed into huge flat lobes an eighth of an inch wide, layered like the petals of a flower. The brown, white, and black stripes on its back glistened iridescent gold as I rotated my hand toward sunrise. Hundreds of beetles clung to the undersides of the plants like overgrown drops of dew. It took some doing to pry the beetle from my finger when I returned it to its flower.

By eleven o'clock, the July heat rose in quivering waves off the sand. The grassland on the fringes of the dunes was half in bloom and half in seed. Less than thirty yards upslope from active dunes, a pair of massive pine trees clung to the stabilized sand that rides up the base of the mountains on the north side. The trees were situated midway up the slope, which curved away around a giant corner. I took refuge in their shade, looked out into the shimmering heat, and picked drill-bit-shaped seeds out of my socks. The head of each seed was half an inch long, attached to a two-inch-long twisted stem with a long flag at the end, perpendicular to the drill bit. If the contraption had landed head down, the flag would have caught the wind, drilling the seed two inches into the ground, planting itself. The disentangled seeds were motionless amid the desiccated pinecones, which lay all around the trees like skeletons, half buried in the mat of needles and sand. A pink and black stone lay at the base of one of the trees, a natural seat. Sunlight filtered through branches and needles, creating intimate scenes. It was the perfect place for a nap.

I dozed off in the still heat, surrounded by the fat buzzing of flying June beetles. When they fly, they dangle precariously in the air, abdomen hanging straight down, head pointing straight to the sky. In order to become airborne, they climb atop an available plant and jump. Gaining altitude is a slow process, and sometimes they get knocked down to jarring landings by taller plants in the way. Undaunted, they crawl to the taller plant, climb to the top, and jump off again, buzzing off into the grassland and out of sight.

A sweet explosion of wings woke me as a hummingbird zoomed by just overhead. Her colors flashed as she was caught by one of the pools of dappled light, and I saw her target: a patch of twenty or thirty trumpet gilia blooming in the broken shadows of the trees. Each slender stalk arched under the weight of between six and ten scarlet flowers, which all hung from one side of the stem. Open flowers were miniature gramophones, longnecked champagne flutes, while the closed flowers hung like bottom-heavy rubies. As the shadows moved with the sun, the pools of light caught individual flowers—translucent desert Victrolas and desert crown jewels.

The hummingbird buried her bill to the hilt in all of the open flowers on each stalk before moving on to the next, leaving few flowers unsampled. When she finished one stalk, she would pop up into the air, hover for a second, and make a choice as to which stalk to try next. Then, like an arrow, she would zip right to the next flower with seemingly effortless accuracy. She worked her way through the patch until she was at the stalk of flowers closest to me, only three feet away. Making quick work of the six flowers on that stalk, she popped up eight feet in the air, suspended between the dead fingers of the lower branches of the pine. She turned three times, looking in three different directions, chose her next target, and zoomed off around the bending slope.

At almost the same second, I flinched sideways as a madly buzzing tangle of black wings and long insect bodies catapulted directly at my head. Two mating robber flies, almost as large as dragonflies, tumbled in and landed in a heap on the bark of the tree next to me. They were attached at the end of their abdomens, joined but facing opposite directions. The combined effort of their flying resulted in the pair's rocketing straight up four feet into the air, buzzing violently, and then falling into a crash landing a second later. Looking downslope for the next half hour, I witnessed dozens of similar flights—tiny fireworks in the grassland, in the pain and joy of creation.

The sun eased behind a cloud and everything went suddenly dark. Raindrops fell softly around me on the sand and in the trees, and on the matted pine needles and in the grasses, and all the way out onto the dunes. I had never understood the term "pattering rain" before, but this was pattering rain. It was just suddenly all around me, and then came a little breeze and the smell of wet sand. But even as it started, just on the next slope, sunlight flooded in behind the tiny rainstorm. Within seconds my surroundings were completely suffused in light. Still the rain pattered on the sand around me,

a desert sun-shower.
Cool drops dampened my face in the warm sun,
bearing the smell and taste and sound
of liquid summer.

After the sun-shower, the wind stopped and the air was still. I took out my camera and long lens, secured them to my tripod, focused on a flower, and waited. A male rufous hummingbird appeared in the patch of gilia, as bright as a medallion in his copper armor. He flew away in a songbird's dipping flight, folding his wings against his body, falling, then catching himself as he opened his wings again. He was followed a short while later by a pair of calliope hummingbirds that tussled near the ground in an indistinguishable flurry. At the conclusion of the battle, the male chose a stalk of gilia and drank from every flower. The female followed right behind him, visiting every flower on the same stalk in the same order. Then they both zipped up to a branch right above my head and sat for mere seconds before another tussle broke out, and they took off again. This time, the female flew first to a stalk of flowers, mining all of them, and the male flew in behind her, hitting each of the flowers in the same order. Then they both whizzed off behind the curve of the hill, snipping at each other.

As the light changed, I refocused the lens on different flowers, hoping for a hummingbird to fly into the frame. I was never without distraction. Every so often a cloud of flies surrounded me and landed on my arms and legs. An elegant wasp with a red back and a black tip on its stinger landed on my arm as well. Its body was blown glass. It held the stinger at the end of its exceptionally long, thin abdomen like a drop of water clinging to a strand of grass. Most of the weight of the insect was up front in its head and thorax, but the stinger and the long abdomen provided the perfect counterweight. Its huge eyes bulged from either side of a sharp beak of a mouth. This was a beast. It rested for a minute and then took flight again, using its raised abdomen and stinger as a rudder.

The heat and stillness bore down on me. The wind started with a gust, riffling through the rabbitbrush and the low-lying grasses. It combed them, and the sound was like a low wooden whistle, changing in half pitches as the gust swerved and spirited through the grasses and out onto the dunes. I got stung by a bee.

And with that the wind came in from behind me and brought everything on the entire hillside to life. Every flower on the slope swayed and dipped. The wind rolled down the mountain in pulses. It would pick up for thirty seconds, whistle through the pine needles, and then die away, leaving the air almost still. Layer upon layer of cool air descended the tall mountains behind me. I shivered and changed into a fleece. Gusts came with increasing frequency, each one colder than the one before. In the distance there was a deep rumble as the sky cleared its throat. I realized that the worst place for me to be was under the two lone massive pines on a high slope with a thunderstorm approaching, so I abandoned my post.

There was stillness in the middle of the storm. There was no wind, so the rain fell straight down, bouncing off the branching strands of Indian ricegrass, making them jump. The same happened with the sunflowers, the first of the season: When a fat drop caught a leaf, it would bounce off and make the plant shudder. And then the wind started again, forcefully, and lightning fingered overhead. The storm was back for real again.

I had retreated into a depression filled with sunflowers and ricegrass near the bottom of the slope. The second wave of the storm lasted more than two hours. The land accepted the rain and the wind that came with it. The entire grassland danced in unison. Wind ripped through the grasses in my trough, pushing them almost flat against the sand and whipping drops of cold rain up under my visor and down the back of my neck. Water streamed off my raincoat. An errant stream pioneered a channel into my coat and down my chest. Soon I was almost as wet inside the coat as I would have been without it, so I stripped it off and embraced the rain.

The performance came in waves. Between them, pockets of silence and stillness punctuated the acts. Then the rain would return, the sky would grumble, and the whole thing would begin again. In some strange way, I had begun to enjoy being cold and soaked. In all, I spent five hours in the depression, saturated by the storm. Finally, around dusk, the last wave rumbled away. The sun slowly peeked out from beneath the clouds, revealing, in twenty seconds of soft veiled light, layers of red-brown dunes tinged with pink, sheets of retreating rain, and swollen green grasses. Silent dripping trees and sunflowers were suspended in time, and the last of the raindrops fell on me and my camera.

Before the storm, the grasses and rabbitbrush had shown dark against the silvery midday dunes, but now the contrast had been reversed. The dunes, dark with rainwater, showed off the bright grass greens of the summer grassland and the bright sun yellows of summer sunflowers. The sun dropped even farther below the stormclouds, and the soft tones and muted layers of rain gave way to deep orange light. Numbingly brilliant twin rainbows appeared with eerie speed, hung in their powerful arcs against the dark clouds and sand. They etched themselves onto the dunes and the sky, vibrating with their own color. The last of the rain hung midway across the dunes, so the rainbows lasted ten minutes, radiant, suspended. Only as the sun dipped below the horizon on the west side of the valley did the rainbows start to fade away from the bottom up. The sky slowly retracted the ribbons and left, at the last minute, a touch of color in the clouds before the sky took back all of its light.

Receding Storm

I switched into my only dry clothes—a down jacket and running shorts—and walked barefoot under the weight of my sodden pack through the wet grasses into the dunes to find a place to sleep. A flying June beetle charged my headlamp, balanced at the edge of physics against the black sky, its eyes reflecting the light with an eerie internal glow. Just after dusk, I found two evening primroses opened to the night, and a moth— a huge hummingbird moth—tasting the secretive flowers.

The next day I started walking an hour before sunrise and resumed my post beneath the two trees by six o'clock. I again trained my camera on the flowers and sat back to watch as light flooded the dunes.

In the distance several Clark's nutcrackers started shrieking all at once, strident and disturbed. The calls were hoarse, indicative of attack mode. Moments later, the assailed, a sharp-shinned hawk, sped by, gliding powerfully along the contour of the hill, down the slope and out into the grassland. The stressed calls stopped.

To keep from getting stiff, I stretched my legs and adjusted my position slightly. A shaft of filtered light caught a different flower and I refocused the lens. And then the most incredible sound reached my ears. From what seemed to be the center of the dunes came a whinnying like a sad, lost colt. The voice was on the verge of a cackle, nearly hysterical. The bizarre call repeated over and over like a restless spirit wailing, bodiless and confused, almost supernatural. Finally the source walked into sight, and it was a bird: a grouse. Maybe it was a lost juvenile calling for food. Or perhaps it was just lonely. It walked by several times, weaving in and out of the grasses. The grouse took a position on a rock that jutted out of the slope, surveying the scene, and called— howling sorrow to the dunes. After ten minutes, it jumped down from its rock and walked off through the grasses, still whining and moaning.

I had just begun to process the experience when a nutcracker landed in the dead lower branches of the pine fifteen feet above me. I jerked my head back to get a good look. My quick movement seemed to scare the bird because it dropped the June beetle it had been eating. The beetle fell directly in my lap. It was missing its head. I brushed the dead beetle off my lap and onto the pine needles. The nutcracker peered down at me.

At the same time, a chickadee flew in somewhere overhead. I could hear it echoing through the trees, chuckling and laughing. The playful calls interwove with the dry-throated call of the nutcracker and the distant wailing of the grouse as it walked away through the deep grasses.

Both the nutcracker and the chickadee flew away moments later, and the strange concert fell into repose. As I watched in the still air, a bloom fell off one of the stalks of trumpet gilia. I sat back, drinking some of the last of my precious water. Every so often a hummingbird would zoom in and work the patch of flowers, but not once did one approach the flower that I had singled out. In fact, the preferred flowers of the day seemed to be the newly blooming white thistles below me on the slope, and not the gilia at all. A gentle breeze mingled in and out of the grasses, testing. Out of the corner of my eye, I saw the headless June beetle move. It shifted, and then miraculously started to creep over the pine needles. I picked it up to find another beetle, a circus beetle, eating from the bottom of the carcass.

The first wind of the morning swept through the trees at half past nine. The sun was moving across the sky, and I watched the intimate scenes changing all around me as the heat again rose off the dunes. A pool of light caught the rock I was sitting on, and a quartz eye winked up at me from one of the crevices.

Hummingbird and Trumpet Gilia

You would think that a huge grasshopper with orange legs and a yellow-green underbelly would be easy to see when you are sitting still. When the insect walks, its red-orange calves are exposed and bright. But when the grasshopper folds its legs and presses them up against its sides, it turns the color of pine needles, pinecones, and sand, and disappears. A chickadee flew back in overhead. I relaxed against the tree, thought about how rare solitude is in our overcrowded world, and felt sad.

I was starting to think about another nap when a female rufous hummingbird appeared in a blurred flurry of wings. She started working the flowers on the outside of the patch. I noted the fluidity and intention of her movement—no wasted energy. I moved my hand into position on the trigger of my camera. Without fanfare, she approached my chosen stalk of flowers. She hung suspended six inches from the flowers and tasted the air with a silvery tongue. My pulse accelerated and I fired off two photographs in rapid succession. The shutter sounds split the stillness like gunshots. She faltered, and snipped at me. She did, however, choose a flower on the stalk and sample it. I fired another two photographs, and these were too much for her. She ducked out of the flower, popped up in the air to snip at me again, then zoomed away.

I apologized with silence as she departed. In the long period of quiet that followed, the only movements were those of the ants and the flies. A layer of black ants cruised over the pine needles, scouring the pine litter, cleaning up and recycling. They started eating the June beetle, which had now been abandoned by the circus beetle. Hardly anything is wasted out here.

As the afternoon wore on, I dozed in broken shade. Sheets of heat siphoned dune ridges into abstraction. The commotion around me had all but disappeared when I suddenly caught sight of a male calliope hummingbird hovering five feet above the ground at a blooming thistle forty feet away. He held his position for a few seconds and then levitated toward me, gaining speed as he left his midair perch. He dipped like a flicker as he closed the distance between us and pulled up into a perfect hockey stop in midair, inches from my face. Each feather of his pink chin shield flashed individually.

The air off of his wings caressed my cheek and blew back my eyelashes—
a delicate reminder
of densely packed evolution,
fending off time
in tiny bundles of whiplike precision,
infused with razor-sharp joy.

Time stood aside. The bird swiveled in a quick, articulate movement and eyed me with one eye. He pivoted on his center of gravity in midair and eyed me with the other eye. He pivoted a third time and pulled out in the same motion, turning and shifting his inertia into forward flight as he zoomed back to the thistle.

I had been sitting under the tree for the better part of two days, waiting for hummingbirds. And now, at least out to the edge of my senses, it truly was still.

Midday Dunes #1

Midday Dunes #2

Sunflower and Shadows

AUGUST: THE SHAPE OF LIGHTNING

The morning was cool and full of dew. Every dune bowl boasted sunflowers in full bloom. Flowers had taken hold in the most unlikely spots. Some grew on windy plains with no other vegetation in sight. Others traced the folds between dunes in strips of yellow. They stood out against darkened sand as the shadows shortened.

I stood alone on the top of a sloping dune, looking out over the world of changing shapes. The sun burned and baked from above and below with equal ferocity, but a ferocity that was somewhat abated by the wind. The deep browns, yellows, reds, blues, and greens of the morning sands had been replaced with a high-sun, washed-out white, the last of the colors visible only on the relatively moist slip faces of the dunes and in the low-lying areas that supported the sunflowers, skeleton weed, blowout grasses, and scurfpea.

The geologic terms used to define sand movement are saltation and repetation. Saltating sand grains catch the wind and bounce along the ground. But it is nearly impossible to see them bounce, and they instead seem suspended in a stream of airborne sand that flows above the dune surface like fast-running water. The repetating grains get their energy from the bouncing saltating grains. They roll and creep on the surface of the dune, under the stream of flying sand. Unlike the saltating grains, the repetating grains move slowly enough that you can follow the paths of individual grains.

I put on a set of clear ski goggles and lowered my head down to the level of the streaming sand. The whole dune surface was moving all around me. The terms of geology aren't intended to communicate the beauty of blowing and creeping sand, either in its power or its rhythm. For that, I would have to resort to poetry, or perhaps interview the circus beetle, which, walking on the windward side of the dune, endured a nearly continual storm of fist-size stones bouncing off the walls of its house.

The most comfortable place in the gale was a ridgetop, on the windward side. The airborne sand on the windy side of the ridge stayed low for the most part, whipping mainly the backs of my calves. As I switched to the leeward side, the air was suddenly filled with sand blowing over the ridge. There was sand down the back of my shirt, in my ears, in my mouth, and up my nose—which, to be fair, had a certain strange charm. But the sandstorm certainly was not good company for eating a peanut butter, honey, and banana sandwich.

The sandwich had melted, of course, which suited me fine. I was enjoying the complex taste when a ladybug materialized out of the sun and sand and swirling wind. The ladybug landed, without apology, on the very tip of the index finger of my right hand, which still clutched my half-eaten sandwich. The beetle seemed impossibly red against the backdrop of bleached dunes.

After eating my sandwich, I sat on the ridge with my back to the wind. I caught sight of movement against the sand. A beewolf, a type of sand wasp found on the dunes, cruised down below on the leeward side of the dune, angling into the wind. Suddenly, it turned directly toward me.

The wasp, I reasoned, was coming after the honey left in my beard. I prepared my mind as I watched the insect's weaving approach, imagining the tiny, barbed footsteps below my lips, the buzzing of wings, and the intricate tickle of its mandibles, and all completely out of sight, hidden by the shape of my own face. But my discomfort grew as the wasp approached—yellow, black, and buzzing—and in the instant between five feet and three feet away, I no longer wanted the beewolf to land. I swept the insect away with my arm, and it was caught by the wind, pushed back down the leeward side of the dune. Its buzz whined in protest, descending with the Doppler effect.

The wasp recovered, and this time the approach was much quicker. The descending tone reversed, climbing quickly into a crescendo, and I brushed the beewolf away again. The buzzing cycled again, and again, and then again. I am embarrassed to say that I kicked a little sand at it on the next loop, and quickly moved twenty feet down the ridgeline and sat back down.

But the beewolf followed my path down the dune and looped in once more. I brushed it away again in frustration, and a gust of wind caught it and took it on a much longer loop. I followed the long arc of its recovery and finally saw what I should have noticed before. All the way down the leeward side of the dune ridge were insects—flies, mainly, but beewolves, too—caught in the backwash of wind and wind-borne sand. For some reason, all the insects seemed to want to get over the ridge, but few were able to do it. The vast majority were engaged in their own loops. The wind and sand flying over the ridge from the windy side was too much to handle, and insects were actually being forced down to the ground, where they would roll several feet down the leeward side, recover, shake themselves off, and try again.

Understanding finally dawned as I turned my attention back to the beewolf, which was closing in for the eighth time. This time I sat calmly, and the beewolf, having used my wind shadow to approach within inches of my chest, went right around me without so much as touching me.

I climbed up the side of Star Dune, one of the largest dunes in the field. The ridge felt nearly vertical, and I had to stop every ten steps, sliding back in the cascades of sand. My thighs burned and sweat stung my eyes. I reached the top on all fours. Star Dune is just that—a star-shaped dune with ridges extending in multiple directions, arising from multidirectional winds. It has three faces, and they meet at the top. On the summit, I dropped my pack and leaned against it.

I didn't rest for long, though, because a golden eagle soared above me, floating over the silvery dunes. I dove into my pack and extracted my camera. The eagle had traveled more than half a mile before I was ready. But even at that distance, the bird was massive and majestic through the lens. It flared, wings nearly perpendicular to the ground. The dunes behind looked like crumpled linen, wrinkling in the rising heat. I took six photographs in quick succession, and then the bird leveled off and flew out of my line of sight.

Clouds started to roil. I napped on the top of Star Dune, my back again to the wind. When I woke, light and shadow were playing hide and seek on the dunes, and the wind had died. I spied a set of sunflowers perched precariously on a saddle below me, so I dropped down. Camouflaged on one of the flowers was an almost translucent green spider. I unpacked my camera and knelt down, engrossed.

Golden Eagle over Midday Dunes

I'm not sure how much time passed, but probably only half an hour. Lightning splintered the air with simultaneous flash and crack. Fat raindrops plopped down at once. The storm had come in from behind Star Dune. My heart beat in my ears. I was way too high on the dune. I stuffed my camera into my pack and zipped it quickly. I pulled the pack onto my back and stood up. But as I did, all of the hairs on my head, neck, arms, and legs shot straight up in the air.

The next few seconds remain frozen in slow motion. The straps of the pack slipped off my shoulders. My left hand caught for a split second, then broke free. I took six accelerating steps, digging my feet into the sand, and dove headfirst down the steep slip face of Star Dune.

There are no words for the sound. It filled everything. Every muscle in my body clenched tight, squeezing adrenaline. Blinding light etched my shadow on the sand to my left. The air sizzled, thick with the acrid stench of ozone. My breath was knocked out of me. I saw red.

Then time seemed to speed back up. I tumbled halfway down the dune, then ran, tripped, and fell on my face. My heart was racing. My temples pulsed with frightening force. I was sure I was going to pass out. I tried to calm down, tried to take deep breaths. My body was covered in cold sweat. I had lost my goggles and hat, and a contact lens had fallen out of one eye. My other eye was full of sand. The pain was excruciating. I popped out the other lens into my hand, and everything was fuzzy. My throat felt raw. Maybe I had screamed. I couldn't remember.

It was raining hard now. Lightning split the sky overhead. My heart had slowed, but every crack made me jump. I regained my breathing and popped the contact into my mouth. Water and sand streamed all around me. I was soaked and freezing cold and had a pounding headache. Everything was sore. I had pulled a muscle in my neck and one of my calf muscles was balled up. It felt like a white-hot rock. My elbows, knees, and forehead were bleeding. The rain turned to hail. I closed my eyes, covered my face, and waited.

I am not sure how long I huddled there, but four waves of the storm came through. I didn't move. I was too cold, too scared, too shocked. It was near sunset when the sky above me finally cleared. Everything grew still. I put my contact back in and limped to the top of the dune to retrieve my pack. The sand was hard-packed with water, almost like cement. I found my hat and goggles half buried on the way up.

My pack was soaked, of course; my sleeping bag useless. I was not carrying a tent. I dropped down to the bottom of the dune again for the night. Luckily, a down coat, rain pants, and rain jacket were stuffed deep in the pack, and they were dry. I changed into them and lay down on my pad to sleep. My whole body felt truly wretched. My ears were still ringing and continue to ring slightly to this day. I had almost been struck by lightning. It seemed ridiculous. Perhaps I was in shock, but the whole thing made me want to laugh. The day seemed faraway and unreal.

I woke before sunrise, even more stiff and sore than I had been the day before. I could only turn my neck a few degrees. I carried only two medicines: aspirin and Neosporin. I took five aspirin and followed them with some trail mix and water. It took less than twenty minutes to return to the top of Star Dune. The climb up was easy, despite my burning calf, because of the hardened sand.

Sunrise from Star Dune

Drying Dunes from Star Dune

I don't think I had ever appreciated a dawn as much as I appreciated the one that morning. The light kissed my face. Shadows and curves and the straight edges of ridges all seemed to make sense in a new way. I just hoped the lightning hadn't fogged my film. The previous day's events seemed almost abstract, as if they had happened to another person.

I laid out my wet clothes and sleeping bag in the sun to dry, weighting them down with my boots and tripod. The shadows of morning were quickly gone, but the dunes remained dark and saturated with water. As the morning wore on, the dunes began to transform. They were drying. First the ridgelines dried, outlining everything with a thin white pencil. Then other patterns appeared—patterns more intricate and sensuous than I had ever imagined.

Everywhere I pointed the camera there were photographs. The sand dried in loops and whirls and zig-zags. Every dune bowl revealed concentric circles of dry and wet sand. Whole plains became striated, showing off their elegant wind-packed cross-bedding. Slip faces unveiled complex fissures in the slumping sand. The story of wind was written in the stillness. The underlying structure of the dunes was exposed.

Convective clouds began to build overhead. I didn't need to be told twice. I packed up my gear and headed down. The ground was still hard and the walking was easy. I decided to cut my trip short and hike out. I didn't feel like sitting through another storm. On the way back I kept looking over my shoulder. The sky was already grumbling.

Halfway back, I stumbled over a whole field of what looked like coyote scat. But there was way too much. Six-inch-long gray artifacts were scattered in a circle 100 feet across. They looked out of place, other-worldly. My spine tingled. They looked like vertebrae. They looked primeval. I knelt down and picked one up. It was feathery light, but seemed solid. The outside felt rough and resembled granite. Irregular fins and grooves spiraled around it. Then I turned it around and my stomach flipped. It was hollow. A tunnel with walls of glazed glass went all the way through the object. I was looking at a fulgurite.

This was a place where lightning had struck the dune. The sand around the current had vaporized instantly into glass tubes, the heat fusing more sand to the outsides. The insides betrayed the shapes of pure lightning, frozen in time. The glass tubing had cooled instantly as well, shattering into sections. All of the fulgurites were hollow. Some were flat and wide where the electricity had spread and flexed. Some were straight with holes the width of a pencil. One was the width of my thumb. Another curved where the electricity had made a sharp turn. Still another was a rope of three thin tunnels braided together. The longest one, more than a foot long, was a bent pipe. All the fulgurites were aligned toward the center of the strike like spokes on a wheel.

The sky grumbled again. I hurried on. Two hours later I was within sight of my car. Rain splattered down. I leaned into my pack, trying to ignore my throbbing calf. Lightning scorched the sky right above me, but I didn't even break stride. I made it to my car just as the hail started pounding down, heaved my pack into the back, and jumped, dripping wet, into the driver's seat. Lightning flashed everywhere and waves of rain lashed at the road. It was impossible to drive. So I pulled off, sat safely in my car, and enjoyed the storm.

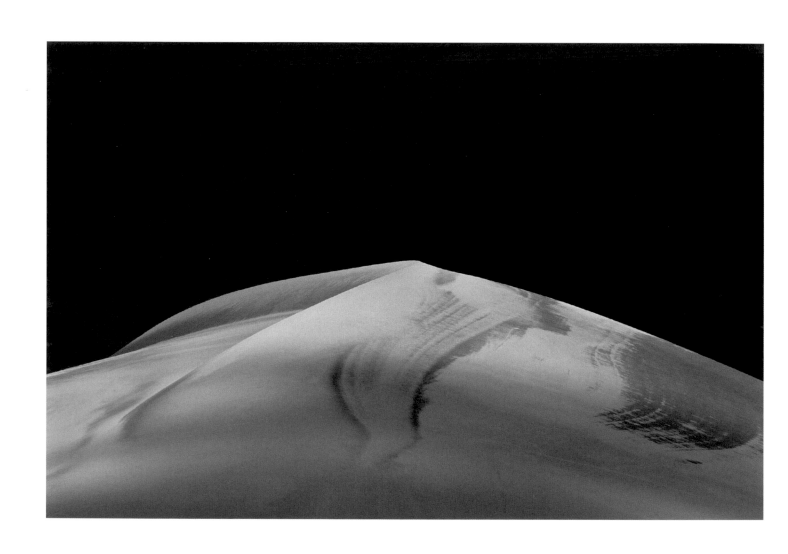

Drying Dune and Shadow

Drying Sand Abstraction

Interwoven Dunes

Sunflower and Spider

SEPTEMBER: THE WIND SENDS FLOWERS

The now-familiar trail around the north side of the dunes held a surprise: bear prints three-quarters the size of my own boot. They looked somehow human—five clearly imprinted toes and an elongated heel pad—but nightmarishly so because of the claws, which curved deeply into the soft, damp sand. The large rear prints registered almost directly on top of the smaller front prints, indicating a slow and easy gait. Even before I had made a close inspection, I could see that the tracks were sharply defined, fresh, almost steaming. The surrounding sage, clinging to the afternoon's rain, smelled of a two-tone, sweet-acrid, wet green. I followed the tracks toward sunset.

I set out my tent in a sand hollow surrounded by looming dunes and looking straight out at Mars, one steady, unblinking light suspended among the twinkling stars of Aquarius. The air was cold, the black fabric of the sky crisply ironed. I sat in the doorway of my tent, imagining NASA's ambassadors, *Spirit* and *Opportunity*, hurtling toward the red planet to perform a 90-day search for water. Tracking facilities in the Mojave Desert, Madrid, Spain, and Canberra, Australia, were receiving messages and sending orders to the two spacecraft as they neared the 17-million-mile halfway point. But that communication was all out of earshot. I could only ponder the vast distances and emptiness of deep space for a few minutes; after that I started to feel homesick.

My eyes struggled against the dark. Except for Mars, the stars, and the deep black sky, everything around me was grainy, darting around in front of my eyes like remnants of the Big Bang. But during the next half hour, shapes slowly resolved themselves, and my eyes focused through the static. Suddenly the dune to my right turned a ghostly, milky white. The light intensified, and the moon came over the far ridge a minute later, dazzlingly bright. The world was again filled with minute detail. Long shadows extended from my tent and my boots and the chest-high bushy sunflower plants growing improbably in the open sand. The largest of the plants branched into fifty-six flowers. With the moon came a gentle mountain breeze.

As the highest peaks cool, dense air sweeps down, flooding into the valley. The intensity of the flow increases throughout the night, but the dunes don't always experience this wind. At times, a layer of stable air descends on the dunes, colder than the air above it. This temperature inversion is like a blanket and pushes the flow of mountain air up into the atmosphere. Stillness on the ground does not translate to stillness 200 feet overhead.

I walked over and examined the sunflowers, trying to see yellow. I could almost imagine the color, like a faded, handpainted black-and-white photograph. The sunflower heads bowed, bobbed, and bumped into one another, swaying in the mountain wind.

I turned my attention to my shadow—gangly legs stretched across the sand, bent like a grasshopper's. When I moved them just right, it looked as though I wore stilts. It had been awhile since I had played with my shadow. I started without thinking. I lifted my knees and danced on the dune in the moonlight. I danced by myself in the clear, silver-gelatin world.

I shed my jacket and boots and ran barefoot on the cold, rippled sand. The sand was so cold that it hurt, but I ran anyway, digging in my toes and pumping my fists. At the top of a low dune, I stopped, gasping cold air, and greeted the moonlight with arms spread wide. My shadow, registered a short distance away on a higher dune, became a pictograph painted on a rock wall, echoing loon calls across a still northern lake. It became a petroglyph etched into the stone in a haunted Utah canyon. With its own brevity, the shadow became supremely, elegantly human. By midnight, my shadow had shortened, I was back in my boots, and I could definitely see the yellow of the sunflowers.

Quite a different wind accompanies sunrise. As soon as the sun heats the surface of the sand, a thin layer of warm air starts to rise, creating an almost immediate, but temporary, low-pressure system over the dunes. The convective currents disturb the higher layer of air, still flowing down the mountains from the night before. The temperature inversion breaks down as the two layers mix, and the result of the turbulence is wind. In the winter, the sunrise wind frosts all of the dune ridges for about two minutes before the warmth of the sun over-powers the wind chill.

Mornings are visceral rhythm: the cold metal of a camera through woolen mittens and smokelike breath in deep blue shadows of predawn; the chill of the sunrise wind and the surprisingly harsh light ten minutes after; rock-hard Clif Bars and a water bottle with the lid frozen shut. Days become rhythm too: the weight of the pack digging troughs into my shoulders; the grinding under my feet as I walk; the sound of the wind and the blasts of sand; the resting and the thinking.

I came across the grave of an elk. Two vertebrae, a tibia, a fibula, and a rib were strewn in a small arc. Four points of an antler stuck out of the sand, still intact, but desiccated, bleached, and sandblasted to the texture of weathered wood. The bones had caught the seeds of sunflowers the year before and now the little patch of flowers, removed from any others, guarded the site. The wind always sends flowers.

I circled the grave, said a silent farewell, and continued, sand again grinding under my feet. The day grew still and bright. Occasional gusts of wind chased each other over the shadowless rolling dunes. On the top of one scoured, rippled dune, a squat brown umbrella of a mushroom grew out of the sand. There was no vegetation within a hundred yards of it.

I set an early camp on the eastern part of the Star Dune Complex in a deep sand bowl, also lined with sunflowers. Star Dune, where I had been in August, is a lone, star-shaped dune near the southern edge of the field, but the Star Dune Complex on the northern edge is a huge lobe of star-shaped dunes. All the ridges of these dunes interlock like a heap of starfish.

The relative stillness ended at four o'clock in the afternoon. I saw the wall of rain approaching long before the wind hit. Dark towers of clouds with no tops governed the sky, which grumbled twice, then split open. Lightning crackled. I scurried the half mile to my tent as pea- and marble-size hail pelted painfully down, leaving welts on my exposed forearms. The hail was ferocious. I had often contemplated the sound of a sand-storm from the perspective of a beetle—the continual barrage of fist-size stones pummeling the sides of its house. Now huddled and dripping in my tent, I was the beetle, and the sound was deafening. I could no longer hear the individual hailstones, only a terrifying rattling punctuated by the slicing cracks of lightning and chest-vibrating booms of thunder.

For all its force, the hail lasted only a few minutes. When it stopped, I emerged from the tent into the cold, whipping rain. To my surprise, the tent, which had shuddered so violently, appeared undamaged. Drifts of hailstones had collected in every lee but were already melting in the rain. Many of the sunflowers had been clubbed down or hung limp and decapitated. Quite a few, however, hadn't been touched. I wondered how the mushroom had fared.

In my haste to get out of the hail, I had dropped a knob off of my tripod head that controls the movement. I had been meaning to fix it before the trip but had forgotten. Without that knob, the tripod would be basically useless, so I retraced my steps up the dune in effort to find it. It was lying where it had fallen at the top, and I pocketed it. The back of the storm was now visible, a thin line of sky stretching across the valley. Huge drops of rain splattered on my face, but thunder rumbled now only in the distance. A new wall, this one of golden light, crept out from under the black clouds. It emerged tentatively, then gained speed, racing across the valley and finally engulfing me in forceful orange, the power of the light equal to that of the storm. The sun directly at my back, I turned to see a rainbow arcing around my shadow, both ends of the arc hitting the dunes with splashes of color. My whole body ached and dripped.

The rainbow lasted only a minute before the sun slipped out of the thin gap of sky and behind the far line of mountains. The bottoms of the black swollen clouds turned blood red, lighting the entire world again like a fanned ember. Everything seemed to pause. Then the after-burn faded as the last of the rain and wind whipped across the dunes. An hour later, I sat in total darkness except for a twinkling line of lights from Alamosa, thirty miles away, and the last of the lightning, which sparked and flashed silently far to the north.

The next day was calm and clear. The predawn smelled wet. I started watching sunflowers at sunrise. I had scooped together the perfect sand daybed and propped myself up on my arms in the midst of a few plants that were on a sand saddle overlooking most of the western edge of the dune field. Amazingly, the hail had hit only one of the group. The dunes on the edge tapered off into a sea of low, stable, vegetated dunes called the Sand Sheet. The Sand Sheet vegetation glowed in the morning sun.

Not moving, I dropped into a deep meditation and slowed my breathing as I concentrated on the sunflowers. The world was so still that it seemed as if it had turned to crystal and I would break it if I so much as twitched. The sky was a great lid locked down on the earth, aggressively blue without a single wisp of a cloud. My eyes traced each leaf and petal, allowing the yellow and green to burn into me, exhausting the cones in my retinas until the image changed colors. My mind slowed to the point at which I could see the sunflowers' shadows moving across the sand, west to east. First they would cross one ripple, then another, then another. Time became palpable. The shadows moved quickly at first, then slowed further and further as they shortened while the sun climbed higher. The heads of the flowers followed the sun, moving in opposition to the shadows.

Everything seemed to stop at midday. The shadows were nearly gone and the flowers pointed straight up. One errant breath of air, surprising, almost shocking in the stillness, brushed my cheek and shook the flowers, which quickly returned to center as the air died again. Then, as the sun started to slide down the other side of the sky, the shadows reappeared, braving eastward as the flower heads continued to rotate westward. A fly buzzed by, swerving around me. The shadows lengthened, again picking up speed. It was three in the afternoon. I had been propped up on my arms, comfortable and motionless, for more than seven hours. There had been just that one hint of a breeze.

Suddenly the crystalline day, the seven hours of stillness, shattered.

Out of the silence came an angry, guttural, sterile, mechanically precise sound—a grating buzzing and grinding. I jumped from prone to standing in a single motion, my head spinning in disbelief. My mind, so rested and unfettered, formed a single word: NO. I half expected the word to stop the noise, to reverse it, but it continued, unrelenting despite my silent anguish. Two people on ATVs were in the park. But where? The sound seemed to be both far away and right next to me, filling all of my senses. Then I saw them. They were just black dots on a dune, distorted by heat and distance. I could see them shooting up and over ridges, hear them grinding down deep as they hit the inclines, releasing their clutches and shifting gears.

Below me on the Sand Sheet, a herd of elk that I hadn't previously seen sprinted to the top of one of the low vegetated dunes and stopped abruptly, their backs to me. All fourteen of them were looking intently toward the noise. All of their ears were pointed forward, and I could see their muscles rippling with fear. They held their position for about ten seconds, then turned and bolted. They ran in panic, one of the adults half trampling one of the year's calves. They ran away from the sound. They ran for their lives.

I watched them run around the front of the Star Dune Complex, more than three miles from where they had started. They were still running when I lost sight of them. Tears of anger and frustration coursed hotly and impotently down my cheeks. I bit the inside of my cheek and spat blood.

One of the ATVs got stuck halfway up a dune, and I could hear the struggling machine digging itself in deeper. The second ATV came back and pulled out the first. Then both of them drove on, jumping another ridge. That horrible angry noise continued off and on for the next half hour as the ATVs tore up the dunes. I thought of the perfect, delicate mushroom. I thought of the kangaroo rat dens and beetle holes and the long, horizontal roots of grasses, just below the sand. I thought of my footsteps, each so carefully placed. I took out my map and figured out exactly where the ATVs were. As the crow flies, they were almost six miles away. My heart was broken.

Night came clear and cold, the air cleaned by the rain and maintained by stillness. I slept outside, dreaming darkly, and woke in darkness, beating the sun by more than an hour. I walked back to the set of sunflowers on the sand saddle, still feeling depressed. But to my amazement, the elk were back. The bull was actually bugling on a dune a half mile away. Then he walked down off of the ridge and into the Sand Sheet, joining the rest of the herd, near the place where they had been the day before when they were spooked by the ATVs.

Hours later, once the herd had disappeared quietly, I followed the bull's tracks up the dunes. He had walked quite far up into the active sand, climbing ridge after ridge. There were new beetle holes and kangaroo rat dens in the troughs between dunes, the piles of excavated sand still drying from the last night's work. The air was crystal clear. I topped the steep wall of sand to stand on the bull's bugling platform, and I found, right there, another little umbrella: the perfectly formed cap of a solitary mushroom.

Sunset Light

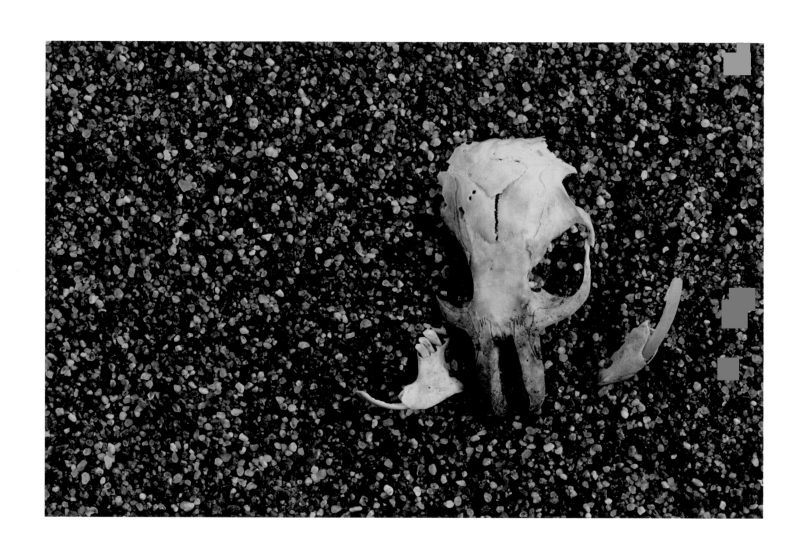

Kangaroo Rat Skull

Slumping Ridgeline

Sunset from the Western Edge of the Dune Mass

Lone Bull Elk

Autumn Cottonwood from an Orphan Dune

Admittedly, I carry quite a lot more than I would need to survive. But even stripped to the bare essentials, I would be a lumbering giant compared to the sleek red fox that I saw on the southwestern corner of the dune mass. I surprised the fox as it hunted deep in a dune bowl, my approach hidden by a gritty wind. The animal was livid red. It took one look at me and then bounded straight up an almost vertical wall of sand. It vaulted the top ridge like jumping over a fence, flipping its tail in the air as it disappeared.

I struggled on in envy. My pack contains: cameras—a Canon EOS-1V, which is gasketed and thus almost impervious to sand; 24mm and 90mm tilt-shift lenses; a 100–400mm lens; a 600mm lens; and 20 rolls of 35mm film. My 4x5 equipment includes a Canham body, a 90mm Rodenstock Grandagon, a 150mm Schneider, a 360mm Nikkor T, a Fuji quickload film holder, 40 sheets of 4x5 film, a darkcloth for the 4x5, a photo-vest, a handheld Pentax spot meter, a 4x loupe for focusing on the ground glass of the 4x5, and cable-releases. I also carry a Gitzo 505 tripod with an Arca-Swiss monoball head, and extra batteries for the camera and spot meter. Joining the camera equipment are: a handheld recorder and tapes for taking notes, extra resealable bags and black tape (for sealing lenses), Band-Aids and Neosporin (for the most awful hangnails of all time), a multifunction tool, toilet paper, and my food for the trip (I usually eat Clif Bars, peanut butter, and salami and cheese on dark rye). Tied to the back of the main pack is a small daypack with sunscreen, a rain jacket and rain pants, long underwear, a down jacket, a wool hat, and gloves. Depending on how close I am going to be to water, I will either strap on one or two water bags. If two, then they hang from the sides of my pack behind my elbows. If one, it hangs down behind, under the daypack, and I add a water filter to the daypack. Strapped to the bottom of the pack are my sleeping bag and sleeping pad, and in winter, my tent. I wear my clothes.

To put on the pack, I stand it straight up and down. Luckily, the sleeping bag, pad, and tent raise the shoulder straps to the right level. I sit down in front of the pack with my legs bent and my hips rotated to the right so that I can rest my knees on the ground. I put on the shoulder straps and the waist belt and lean backward against the pack. I hold that position for a second, then release the backward pressure and explode forward, tightening my stomach while reaching behind my head to pull on the top handle of the pack with my left hand. If all goes well, I roll onto my knees with the pack on my back. Standing up is also a bit tricky because it involves shifting the weight of the pack up on my back so that I can straighten my legs. More than once, I have failed in one of these steps and found myself on my back like a turtle.

This time, as I pulled on my pack, which at the moment weighed more than a hundred pounds, I heard a pop and a tear. One thing that I have learned by spending a lot of time hiking around with that much weight is how to repair my pack with rope and duct tape.

Sand Creek runs nearly year-round on the northern edge of the dune mass. For many of my past trips, I had started on the northern edge and walked around the dunes until I hit the creek. This trip, I walked south to north along the western edge of the dune mass, intending to reach Sand Creek three miles farther downstream. I was carrying only enough water to get to the creek. I walked the line between the dunes and the Sand Sheet, where the yellow flowers of rabbitbrush flow up and over the pleats of low dunes to the west, a sea of gold. The ecosystem exists in a thin layer between sand and sky, stretched literally like a sheet across the low dunes, anchoring and stabilizing them with an immense system of roots. It is punctuated every so often by the glare of active sand on clean, orphaned dunes, miles from the main dune mass—tears in the thin sheet of life. As the Sand Sheet approaches the main dune mass, more and more of the low dunes are clean sand, and the golden rabbitbrush is confined to the hollows between. When the steep walls of sand start in earnest, the rabbitbrush is all but left behind as the dunes climb skyward.

Exhausted, I rested after forty minutes of movement, surrounded by slow autumn. I had worked my way more than halfway along the front of the dune mass toward the creek. There are two distinct states to every trip I take on the dunes. The first is movement, soaked in a combination of the changing landscape and physical struggle. I admit that there are times when the processes of my own body become overpowering. Each muscle cries out individually with a different demand. But even in concentrated movement, I maintain awareness enough to choose a respectful line of travel. I avoid all the beetle holes and kangaroo rat burrows. It only took one experience of hearing my sliding boots ripping grass roots to learn not to walk on grassy slopes in the dune field. And even in exhaustion, after nine hours of hiking, I am often stopped, as the landscape reaches out to me with dumbfounding beauty.

Then, I enter stillness as if dropping into a cool stream on a hot day. Time slows. Awareness swells, sharply refocusing its lens, and I learn. This afternoon, bees visited each of the yellow sunflowers that still bloomed in October, proving that the commonplace is only an expression of complexity. The bee tends its own food and the sunflower employs its own gardener. The bee moved on and the sunflower remained, unleashing oxygen. I leaned back on my hands and took a deep breath of sweet air, tasting the perfume, connecting myself into the web, releasing my ego into the dunes through my palms. I was back. The darkness came with dead still air and an almost full moon, so I slept the first night without a tent and swept sand under the hood of my sleeping bag as a pillow.

In the morning I heard gunshots echoing across the Sand Sheet, from which direction I don't know. Predictably as I walked through, I found ATV tracks and a gun shell, a Remington .32 Winchester Special. It is illegal to hunt here. It is also illegal to ride an ATV. I put the casing in my pocket. Several days later when I went home, I would glue it to the top of my plywood desk. A dried sunflower would then extend from the two-inch-tall vase in place of the bullet.

After another half day of walking along the edge of the golden ocean, I reached a point where the high dunes cut sharply east. There, a great bay of the Sand Sheet, bordered by active dunes, has pushed its way into the dune mass. Across the bay to the northwest lie the huge woven dunes of the Star Dune Complex. Sand Creek flows beyond the star dunes, so, rather than follow the edge, I turned northwest to cut across the wide mouth of the Sand Sheet bay.

Deep in the golden brushy folds, I looked up quickly. Coming over the ridge I had heard a compound sound—a cross between a stutter, a sputter, a whisper, and a whistle. Two pronghorn bucks stood at attention on the top of the next fold. One of them sputtered again, and the other one whistled high. We eyed each other. The sputterer walked toward me, trying to get a better sense of what I was. He puttered and sputtered, but softer this time, more in question than alarm. He paused and then bounded back to stand with the whistler. They puttered and sputtered softly to themselves and to me, questioning still, and I turned and walked away, downslope into a crease in the low vegetated dunes. A minute later, I emerged from the hollow on the uphill slope of the next folded dune. The pronghorn had held their position to watch me, still not sure if I was any danger. But as I continued my course away from them, they let me pass without comment and went back to eating.

The vegetation stretched outward toward the horizon of imagination, brushing the memory of a land untouched by industrialization, where the next break in the prairie was the Rio Grande. Even now, almost as far as the eye could see was the wild white-gold haze of flowering rabbitbrush, waist high and glowing with seething warmth and radiant light. Step by step, the sea of vegetation revealed itself, textured intricacy. Seven pintails shot by 200 feet overhead, en route to one of the San Luis Lakes, secret jeweled wetlands less than five miles from the desert dunes. The wings whistled above me and above the thousands upon thousands of tiny animal tracks winding their way through the rangeland.

Cricket tracks, like dainty tractor-treads,
and the Jurassic tracks of songbirds,
jumping and scratching,
bouncing along for twenty feet before taking wing.
Mice tracks,
racing, racing, racing on familiar trails,
and kangaroo rats,
more adventurous, but still respectful
of red fox, crisscrossing, infiltrating.
A coyote highway, over a foot wide,
with hundreds of tracks heading in each direction, purposeful.
And, of course, pronghorn tracks, toes spread wide,
grazing in secret hollows
as the now distant sand of active dunes
wrinkled and rippled behind the radiant heat of the stillness.
And then, walking up the next ridge,
the rabbitbrush thinned and fell away,
replaced by Indian ricegrass,
blowout grass, and scurfpea.
I had stepped back out onto the clean sand of an orphaned dune.

Elk Tracks #1

Elk Tracks #2

At the end of the second day I set up camp a half mile from the creek, hidden in the low mounds of dunes to the west of the Star Dune Complex. The moon was full that night, and the massive dunes stood gleaming and still. Coyotes howled and yipped as I fell asleep. I woke up to the first of the morning sounds and the last of the night sounds: the hooting of an owl and the twittering of juncos.

I started walking toward the creek an hour before sunrise. The air was chill and dry, and it stung my cheeks and sinuses. My breath was smoke. The shadows of night subsided slowly at first, and then more and more quickly, revealing their secret. Elk tracks were everywhere. I walked over a great seventy-five-foot-wide swath of tracks—interwoven trails of deeply set hoofprints and the two-foot-long parallel lines of toenails dragging across the sand between tracks. The sand was littered with tracks, tracks on top of tracks, and tracks on top of that. There were tens of thousands of them. Fresh elk scat was scattered over the sand and in the grasses. At the top of a low dune a quarter mile from the creek, I looked east. Impossibly long beams of buttery light were already streaming over the mountains and out into the sky. As I watched, the top of one of the blue darkened dunes caught one of the rays and turned orange. I counted no fewer than twenty other great swaths of elk prints crisscrossing the lowlands and even winding their way up into the high dunes, over massive ridges and out of sight. I had stumbled right into the middle of elk territory and was suddenly aware of every sound that I was making. The two zipper-pulls on my pack were clinking against each other, and the metal on metal sound seemed too mechanical for the morning, so I dropped my pack and wrapped one of the pulls with a piece of duct tape to dampen the noise.

Almost as soon as I had set down my pack, the bugling drifted out across the dunes. The bugle of a bull elk is an ancient sound, and it resonates instinctually like a repressed memory. For such huge animals, their call is surprisingly delicate, starting almost like a high-pitched wheeze. As it builds in volume, the pitch falls, and then, at the bottom note, it is cut off abruptly, and the remaining part of the call is a deep-throated chugging— a deep, wet horn. The bugle sounded twice from the direction of the creek as sunrise warmed me.

I moved on slowly toward the creek. The cottonwoods stood in various stages of yellow, partially hidden behind a high bank of sparsely vegetated sand. I was almost to the top of the high bank when I stopped in my tracks. I could just see the herd across the creek under the cottonwoods at the bottom of the sand gulch. They had not yet seen me. I slowly backed down and worked my way along the outside of the high bank until I got to a better place. I crawled slowly on all fours to the top of the bank and took up post on a dune mound fifty feet above the creek, the entire western edge of the dunes stretching out behind me. A scraggly cottonwood tree grew on top, out of the sand, and served amiably as a backrest. Below me, the creek gurgled slowly in its channel, only inches deep but intensely blue with the reflection of the sky. The elk were now 200 yards downstream and still had not seen me. The bull bugled again, and this time the call rang crystal clear, filling the spaces between the leaves of all the trees in the gulch, reflecting off the water and off the sides of my imagination.

They were moving upstream through the cottonwoods, shadows in the shadows. They moved smoothly right underneath me, twenty-three in all. Two younger males seemed to be free agents, going out ahead of the rest of the herd, but the females and calves stayed clustered. The bull was in the middle but near the back, walking heavily under his gleaming rack of antlers. Just upstream from me, they crossed the creek, splashing through the low water, a few lowering their heads to get a drink. One of the females was a little slow, and the bull asserted his dominance, lowering his head and trotting around her to push her onward. He asserted it again when one of the subordinate males got too close to one of the females. The bull was more menacing in this interaction, and the younger male actually bounded up the bank and trotted off into the dunes, snorting. The second subordinate male followed the first without prompting, leaving a second fresh, deep trail through the fields of other elk tracks. I watched the sacred ritual from the shade of the cottonwood until the herd disappeared around the next curve of the creek.

It was now hot in the sun, but still cold in the shade, so I stretched out on my side on the sand with my face in the shadows and my legs in the sun. I was surprised to find more mushrooms growing out of the sand — two groups of three and one group of two, perfect umbrellas. The bark on the lower branches of the cottonwood hung in strips, limp in the still air. A red-tailed hawk flew along the creek channel, almost at eye level, and swooped in for a perfect landing on the high branch of a cottonwood on the creek, folding its wings, leaning forward and dipping its tail. It slowly faded into the tree. A caterpillar with a gray body covered in fine white hair undulated past me on the sand. Shadows shortened out in the dunes. The breeze started and I rolled over on my back to watch the leaves of the cottonwoods flash in the wind. I slowly shifted as the shadows moved through the day, making sure not to disturb the mushrooms. Now and then, I could hear a whisper of a bugle from up the creek.

In the afternoon, I paid my respects to the creek and filtered a gallon of water. Farther upstream, water runs crystal clear over tightly packed stones, each apparently tapped into place like a cobbled street. But even here, three miles downstream, where stones were few and the channel mostly sand, the water was surprisingly unclouded. A maze of standing and fallen cottonwoods presided over the bottoms surrounding the creek. Dried leaves and fallen twigs crunched underfoot.

There was a ragged tenaciousness to the trees in the bottom. They had obviously been tested by the sand. Fallen branches had been stripped of bark and bleached like giant bones. The living trees looked haggard, standing guard over their fallen brethren, strips of bark hanging from the branches and trunks. The sand around many of the trees was a myriad of elk tracks and daybeds. I felt eyes on me. Sure enough, I turned to look across the creek and found a wide yellow set looking back at me from the crook in a branch of one of the cottonwoods. The owl looked at me intently, and I knew by the body language that it was deciding whether or not to fly. It lifted its tail and shot out a long white stream of guano. It fidgeted on its perch and dipped its head at me, questioning. Not wanting to disturb the bird into flight, I turned and walked slowly back the way I had come. A comfortable distance downstream, I left the creek to the owl and crawled back up the slope and out onto the dunes.

I lay out on the grassy sand to watch grasshoppers. I stretched out on my stomach with my chin atop my folded hands, eyes six inches off the sand. The grasshoppers were the same as the one I had seen in July, walking and showing off their bright red rear calves. When they stopped, they folded their back legs doubled over against their sides, hiding the colorful display and returning to the color of sand. They were in an amorous mood, and over the course of the afternoon I witnessed more than ten pairs mating. At one point, a grasshopper flew in and landed abruptly on the back of my right hand. I lifted my head a bit to see it more clearly. Almost immediately, it started eating my hair. It pulled the hairs into its mouth greedily with its mandibles, and there was the faintest rasping noise as it chewed. It ate the first one down to a stub and then found another one. I don't know if it was the hair itself or the suntan lotion that I had just applied that was the real treat, but the grasshopper went through three whole hairs in short order. It was an odd sensation to watch an insect consume part of my body. I was caught between fascination, discomfort, and an odd sense of connection. Near the end of the third hair, the grasshopper pulled too hard. I had had enough, so I blew it off the back of my hand and onto the sand, where it trekked off into the grasses, displaying its calves.

The sun dropped below the horizon and lit all of the horsetail clouds from across the valley to right above my head. They turned the most exquisite color of hot orange, which deepened until it was dark red, and then faded into soft pinks and purples. Color had not yet gone from sunset when the moon rose, a day past full, on the other side of the sky, shrouded in clouds. I stood on one of the swaths of thousands of tracks, dizzied by the pairs of long, sweeping scores in the sand punctuated by soundly planted impressions of hooves. I listened to the songbirds singing their evening songs as the stars poked out from the darkening sky. I walked the line between day and night with a shadow from sunset on my left, and a moon shadow on my right, barely visible. The moon slowly took over the sky, and my moon shadow grew stronger as sunset finally faded. I hadn't taken a single photograph the entire day.

I crossed over the first swath of tracks and then, heading in the vague direction of my camp, I came across another field of tracks. The interweaving trails told more dizzying stories, and for a moment I could feel the raw power of the herd, hear the snorting and bugling, smell the musk and sweat and hair. I can only imagine the great herds of buffalo tramping across the Great Plains. More wisdom has been forgotten than has been remembered. I crossed the second swath and finally found a set of tracks with my own familiar gait, and these I followed for a mile back to my tent, where I made and ate a slightly sandy cheese and salami sandwich by moonlight.

Bull Elk and Dunes

Snowstorm at Sunset #1

I thought that the ATV tracks stretching out toward the west were more of the same that I had seen in September and October. I felt the hot anger and impotency course through me again. But I found out later that someone had committed suicide on the dunes. The tracks had been made by the recovery vehicle. Then I felt a little ashamed at my initial anger. I can only imagine the man walking out to die and the shadow that must have hung over everything, obscuring even his own beauty. I didn't know him, but I now think of him when I recall the next day's experience.

The dunes were cold and still in early afternoon. Shifting gray clouds had hidden the sun for most of the day, flat light muting the curving layers of tan dunes. I had spent most of the day moving to keep myself warm, pounding my way up to the top of dunes, running down the loose sand walls. I rested my knees three quarters of the way up a large dune in the middle of the dune field, sinking myself into a comfortable sand chair. I was completely surrounded by sand as the performance started with a sudden drop of fifteen degrees. A microburst of cold air was sinking, cooled and weighted down with an invisible load of ice—winter's equivalent to a thunderstorm. The air seeped in and filled every dune bowl, moving so slowly that the massive wall of frigid air barely disturbed the sand. I didn't even know it existed until it was right on top of me. At the edge of it, there was an instant when my eyelashes were frozen and my back was still warm before the cold flooded around me.

Many things on the dunes seem to happen instantaneously, with flurry and flash, but the snow was methodical. The bottoms of the clouds bulged, then started peeling away in fine layers. Snow hung suspended, veiling the mountains. A dusting of flakes appeared on the farthest dunes, silently transforming each ridge and hollow as the storm slowly unfolded.

Snow came as a solid wall but fell softly. Huge rafts of interlocking flakes floated heavily downward like downy feathers. Trickles of even colder air fell faster than the falling snow, racing toward the ground, splashing on the sand. The path of each trickle was revealed by the falling flakes as they pirouetted in the wake. Snowflakes landed softly on my woolen mittens, echoing infinity, validating joy.

> *Powder on the dunes.*
> *White snow tumbling on dry brown sand,*
> *subtlety in high soft light.*
>
> *Interlocking clusters of feathery flakes,*
> *tiny tumbleweeds,*
> *winter's cottonwood cotton.*

The snow stopped as quickly and gently as it had started, and I caught a last glimpse of the storm as it swept its long dress off the dunes and down into the valley. I wished I'd had a microscope, and a thousand years to spend with each thousandth of a second. The dunes were left still, blanketed in white, save the accents of yellow blowout grass and Indian ricegrass, which were sprinkled in the lowlands. I looked out into the center of the dune field. From my feet to as far as I could see, the rafts of tumbleweed snowflakes lay on the ground in quiet anticipation—in stillness, but stillness in motion—a pivot point in the dynamics of atmospheric pressure. Even in the silence, the cold air carried on a running conversation with the snow. There seemed to be almost a murmuring, latent excitement, potential energy, like the stirring and rustling of a marsh just before the predawn, before the first wren lets fly song from the cattail cathedral.

And then the first gust of air, high pressure, came in from behind me, low on the dune, just glancing off the sand below me, folding the thin layer of tumbleweed snow back on top of itself and pulling an undertow of the same, exposing brown sand, and streaking the snow like a dry brushstroke.

The same gust, redirected by the dune, dipped and splashed into a dune bowl, knocking the snow off of clumps of yellow grasses, kicking up snow and rolling across the sand for a second before launching off a low ridge. The same gust bounced again and again, moving away from me all the way down into the heart of the dunes, into the very center of the field. The memory of each meeting of wind and dune was recorded in streaking patterns of snow and sand, a unique sweep of that same dry brush.

And swiftly, the entire dune field was a canvas. The next gust came, and then the next, and then there were ten at once, each leaving an individual track. And then there were thirty at once—a symphony—dry brushes with thin white paint, playing, dancing, repainting the dunes.

Zephyrs whipping, dipping, diving, skipping, ruffling, riffling,
swerved and swept dry snow across the sand,
while the dust-devils waltzed, spinning up and landing gently.
Whirlpools of snow and sand and living breath
flowed up over the crests of dunes, clicking heels: the spirits of the ridges.

The patterns of brushed white tumbleweed snow and dry brown sand were visual memories
of fluid fractals—complexity layered on complexity layered on complexity;
fleeting, rhythmic paintings of reflected music
reclaimed just offbeat with creation.

Tears ran freely, freezing on my cheeks,
my eyes wide, language forgotten.

And then there were five gusts at once, then two, and then just one gust painting the dunes, balancing pressure. But that gust must have just overbalanced the pressure because there was one last gust. While all of the air had been flowing away from me into the center of the dunes, the last gust came back toward me. It was only a breath of air, a sigh, and it only just caressed the now fully repainted scene. With a final puff, it spent the last of its energy on two tiny whirlpools that knocked the snow off seven clumps of yellow blowout grass in the trough below me and was gone. Complexity became simplicity. Everything was complete. The air was perfectly still.

The only sound was the echoing beat of my own heart.

ATV Tracks and Fox Prints

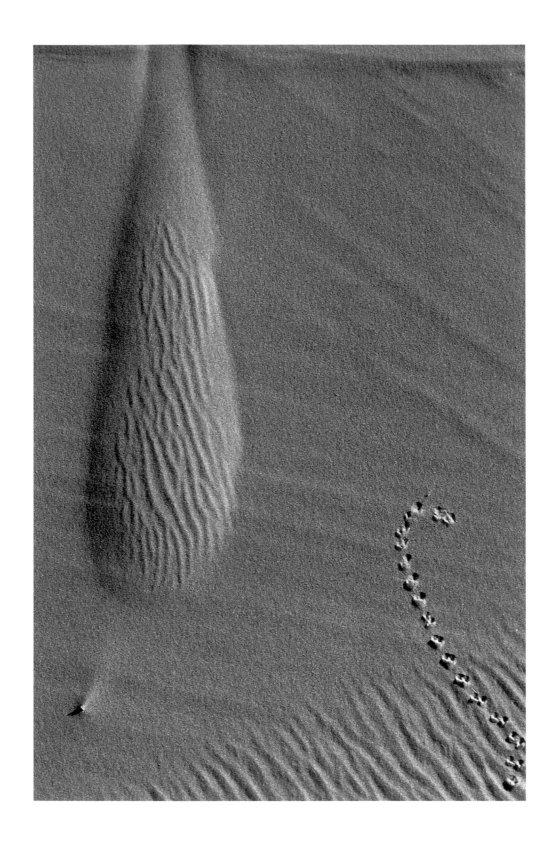

Rippled Slide and Tracks

Snowstorm at Sunset #2

Snowstorm at Sunset #3

November's Blooms

DECEMBER: THE COLD

I was late for work. I had camped in a dune bowl near the western edge of the dune mass, and the night had been hard, cold. At five o'clock, the thermometer read five degrees below zero. I did not know how low it had gotten during the night, but my two-and-a-half-gallon water bags were both frozen almost solid. So when my alarm rang two hours before sunrise and I looked at the mercury, I decided to sleep an extra half hour. When I finally did rise and exit the tent, it was only an hour and fifteen minutes until sunrise. The sky had already gone pink. The entire world glowed from reflected light, some of the richest I'd ever seen. I knew that the light would fade too quickly to photograph, so I just walked and enjoyed.

By midmorning it was almost warm, and I stopped for breakfast. Patches of snow traced the shapes of the shadows, revealing every nuance of the dune slope—mathematical functions of sand, wind, and sun. The deeper shadows held up to six inches, but some snow still clung to areas that lay in shadow for only a few hours per day. Thousands of songbird tracks were interwoven along the outsides of the snow patches, as if the birds had been following a frothing surf line on a beach. Sweeping arcs connected track to track. The trails were almost musical—a curve on the right, a curve on the left, wing marks on the sand.

Everything was raw and exposed. Hummocks of dune grasses, bursting at their sides, displayed tangles of hairlike roots. Sixty-foot-long runners, usually buried just below the surface and connecting many different plants, lay out on the bare sand. Dried sunflowers stuck out of the dune like candelabra. Some of the dried stalks exhibited the results of one of the previous summer's storms. When the plants are still growing, they can sometimes survive being partially excavated by a storm. The winds of a big storm can move many vertical inches of sand, leaving some of the sunflowers' roots exposed. Left without support, the flowers flop over. But if enough roots remain underground, the flower can reinforce the exposed roots and pull itself skyward again. The stems tell the tale with a distinctive S-curve.

The dunes themselves were bunkered down for the winter. In the summer, the ridges are sharp and defined, only a sand-grain wide at the peak. Most winter dunes have no real ridges at all. In winter, the top layers of sand are mixed with snow. I call the mixture "snowstone." The snowstone freezes, thaws, and slumps, collapsing the once-sharp ridgelines into thirty-foot-wide boulevards.

Even in the absence of the snaking ridgelines, the shapes of winter dunes are anything but dull. On the sides of dunes, slumping snowstone rumples and buckles whole boulevards into series of troughs. The wind finds each crease and funnels through it, accentuating the trough into a deep chute with a long wind-tail. Summer's sharp ridges look like folded paper in winter. Each fold is unique, and almost any formation found in Utah's canyonlands can be found in miniature on the broad, crumpled ridges of winter dunes. The miniature formations are sharply defined. The snowstone is honed into buttes, mesas, and canyons. The dunes themselves are reproduced at a 1:500 scale. I have seen textbook examples of star dunes, with their many ridges; barchan dunes, curved convex into the wind; and transverse dunes, long and meandering—all less than a foot tall. The wind, frost, sun, and sand mimic the geology of the entire western desert.

I hiked high into the dunes. Steam rose up as the sand heated in the sun. I stopped, panting, on a ridge affording a view of the whole scene. Far below, grasses and rabbitbrush grew in green-yellow clumps, each protecting a patch of snow. Light coursed over the dunes as the sun moved in and out from behind sporadic clouds. The mountains were pure white against the blue. Oddly shaped islands of snow lay in the middle of the sand—no shadows in sight. Some of the spots of snow lay on fully exposed south-facing slopes. It seemed impossible that they received enough protection from the sun to make it through the day. The islands traced out mysterious patterns on the dune, serving as reminders that I had only the barest inkling of the magnificent forces at play all around me. Suddenly the air was filled with music. Four birds flew by below me. Even in winter, the place had a voice.

Behind me, sunk between three of the high dunes, was a deep dune bowl. Yellow grasses descended into it, clinging to each other. Their combined roots had stopped enough sand movement to create terraces going down one side of the bowl. I could not see the bottom. I stepped down from one terrace to another until I could see into the depths. There, almost forgotten in the pocket, was an island ecosystem. The entire night's activities of a family of kangaroo rats was engraved in the sand. Tracks fanned out, zigzagged, twisted, and braided together through the grasses and dried sunflowers. But each of the trails looped back to the burrow.

From the bottom of the bowl, I couldn't see any of the dunes that surrounded it, only the smooth curve of the slope, posing as an uninterrupted ridge. It was remarkable to me that the kangaroo rats had congregated in the hidden pocket. Even more surprising was that the predators had found the place, too. Circling the bowl were sixteen coyote trails. Rat tracks were registered on top of older coyote tracks.

Suddenly, I was surrounded by songbirds. They descended in a wave, 300 or 400 of them. They moved like water, like dried leaves, like a school of fish. The chattering and chirping was uproarious. I stood still. They walked, jumped, scratched, and flew all around me, eating the seeds from the dried sunflowers. Some of them landed within a few feet of me. Then, without warning, they all lifted off at once, flew over the smooth curve, and disappeared into the clear blue.

Halfway up one of the sides of the bowl, the tops of surrounding dunes came back into view. The sky leaked onto the sand between a dune and the lip of the bowl, the dune floating in the mirage. At the top, I could see clouds rolling over each other south of Blanca Peak. I lay out in the sun, warm on the sand in December, surrounded by islands of snow.

Clouds clogged the western sky, so I thought that the sun would slip away without comment. But the sunset was one of the best ever, with huge plumes of pink on a background of robin's-egg blue. The source of this display, deep orange, slowly drained the color from the sky, concentrating and saturating the center into a deep red. Then, almost at the point where it was gone, the light found another hole and shot some rays back out into the sky: a second sunset. I walked back to the tent in the falling darkness and building wind.

Sunset from the North Side

Second Sunset from the North Side

The first storm tried to come in from the south before sunrise. Blanca Peak, standing like a matriarch, turned it away, sending it across the valley. The second storm came from the west, with strong steady winds, and no mountain to divert it. It hit in midmorning. The windchill plummeted well below zero.

Huge flakes crashed into the sand, pulverizing into a fine white powder. The powder was picked up by the wind, giving it substance as it traced the contours of the dunes. Thousands of the exquisite white streamers fanned out over the sand. The storm was pure exhilaration. I photographed as much as I could, but it was atrociously cold. Twelve minutes into the storm, I tried to take a sip of water from the water bottle that hung at my side. It had frozen solid and cracked. I lost all the feeling in my feet. It felt like I was walking around on stumps. I jumped around, trying to force blood down my legs. An hour into the storm, and my hands were too cold to hold a camera. I fought with the zipper to get in the door of my tent, finally opening it with my teeth. I lay in my sleeping bag, rubbing my numb feet and hands. Then they weren't numb anymore, but painful. Several hours passed before I began to feel warm again.

During the waiting, the wind subsided and the snow began to accumulate. It came down hard, and when I exited the tent again, there were three inches on the dunes. At the same time the day before, I had been stretched out on the warm sand. Now it was three degrees. My hands and feet were still throbbing, but I could see a small break in the clouds and gambled on it. The sun did hit the spot, and there was lukewarm light for several minutes at sunset.

The wind came again during the night and the temperature dropped even further. I tossed and turned, shivering and dreaming of coyotes. When I woke, the wind was steady out of the northwest. It had blown the tops of the ridges clean. Fins of sculpted snow extended on the leeward side of every obstacle, defining the wind-shadows in white. On the leeward sides of the ridges, sand-covered snowdrifts masqueraded as hard-packed sand. I stepped out on one of the drifts and immediately sank knee-deep in soft-packed snow. The edges of the piles revealed layering like picture jasper. The story of the storm had been recorded perfectly, if only I could have read the language.

A small group of horned larks flew by, fighting the wind. They landed below me at the base of the dune, where skeleton weed and Indian ricegrass stuck out of the snow. They floundered, sinking and sliding. Then they took off again into the wind and flared out in a fast arc, quadrupling their speed as they flew back the way they had come. Ravens were out, too, flying fast over the center of the dunes. I saw one with a missing feather on its left wing. The feeling again left my feet, so I abandoned the picture jasper snowdrifts and returned to the tent. Besides, I was out of film.

The storm finally blew itself out that night, and the moon shone bright and cold. I dreamed again of a coyote standing between me and the full moon, casting a shadow on my tent. The dream was so vivid that I could almost smell the animal, hear its breathing. I drifted back to sleep and woke in the morning with my contacts frozen in their case. The contact solution was frozen in its bottle. The water was all still frozen, too. My sleeping bag was frozen from my breath. All I could think about was getting out of the dunes and eating tacos at Taqueria Calvillo in Alamosa—pulled pork and six types of homemade salsa. I was weary of the cold. But I roused myself to greet the sun, and found coyote tracks all around my tent in the snow.

Blowing Snow

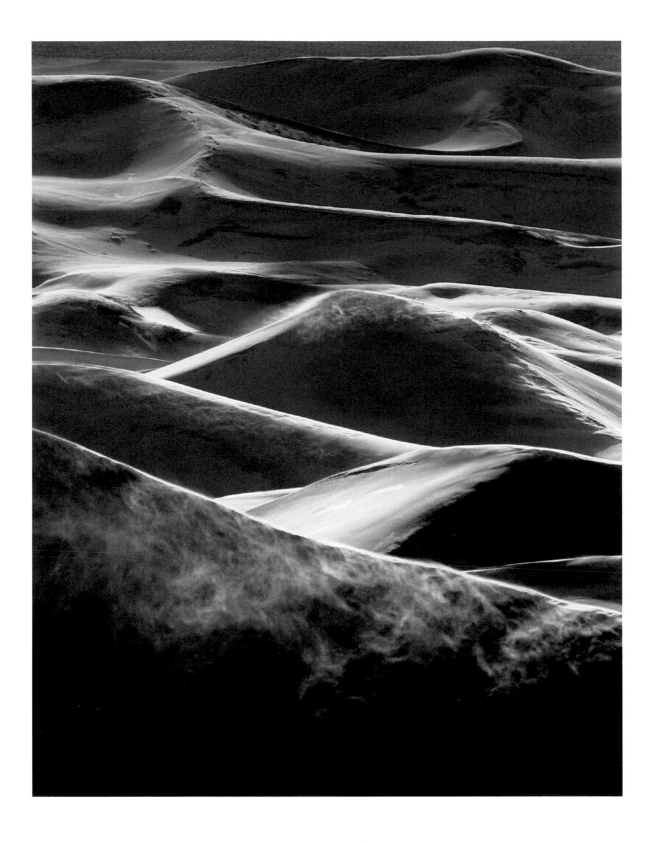

Blowing Sand

Layered Snow and Sand

Miniature Dunes on a Winter Ridgeline

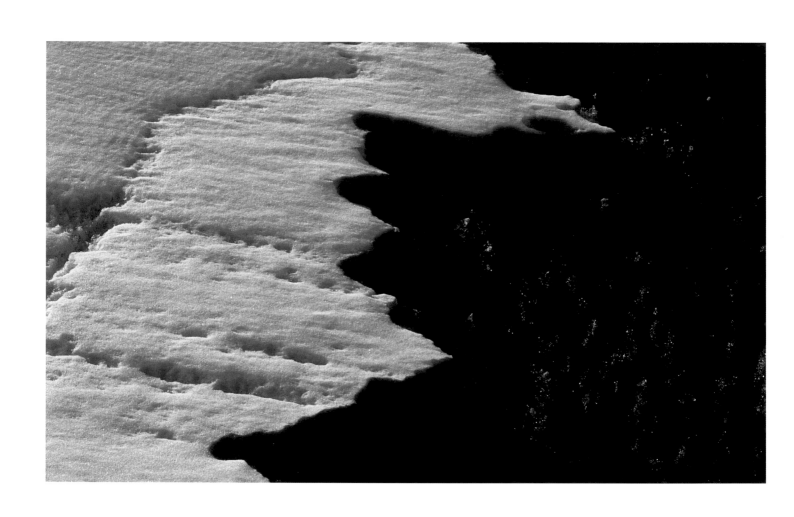

Snow Detail

Horned Lark Fighting the Wind

JANUARY: ORION'S FALL

I found out too late in the frigid dusk that the sand was frozen, slick as ice on the steep face of a high dune. I had made my way halfway across a traverse, only to discover that the route would require crampons and pickaxes. The sand was too solid to kick in even the toe of my boot. I clung to the side for a minute, feeling the weight of the pack, judging my chances. Then I admitted defeat, sat down, and slid 200 feet to the bottom of the slope, taking a long line of snow with me. I finally stopped in a low-lying grassland island surrounded on all sides by the sand sea.

In the morning, the sun was alone in the sky. Glazed snow, sheets of sheen, varnished the dunes. The last week's storm had left eighteen inches. But the dunes were quickly digesting snow, eating away at it from ragged margins. The ridges, heated and scoured by sun and wind, had slumped, flowing in mudslides over the lower snow like drooping elephant skin. Small holes in the snowfields enlarged as the wind picked up sand and bombarded the surrounding snow.

Standing beyond the edge of the disappearing snowfield with the wind at my back, I witnessed the procedure. At my feet, dry sand moved unobstructed, though small spots of wet sand showed where snow was melting underneath. Farther away, dark wet sand became predominant, slowing the progress of the blowing sand. Even farther, the snow became visible, sticking up through the wet sand. Those transitional areas comprised a patchwork of textures—thousands of rows of six-inch-tall shark's teeth, whale's baleen, spines of a deep-sea fish, cracked blisters, chocolate ice cream with freezer burn, Swiss cheese, alligator skin. At the end of the line was the snowfield itself, with ten inches of snow still left in the shadows.

I walked into the sharks' teeth, leaving deep footprints in the sand-covered snow. Upon closer inspection, each of the teeth was an intricate ice sculpture, pitted and cratered by the wind's artillery of sand. On the edges of the structures, tiny beads of ice hung at the end of hair-thin extensions, so fragile that they melted under my breath, crumpling in on themselves.

At the edge of the snowfield proper, I sat at an angle to the sun. The ice sculptures caught the light and sparkled as far as I could see. The reflected highlights were in constant motion as the sun heated the field, melting the delicate structures before my eyes. A faint breeze stirred the dangling husks of Indian ricegrass. I could feel the cold air sweep away the heat radiating off the snow. It was just cold enough to stiffen the ice sculptures and quiet the motion of the sparkles in the melting snow.

At midday the air was warm enough for shirtsleeves. I walked on the northern edge of the dunes, where a steep mountain slope drops like a long ramp from white peaks. High on the slope, twisted junipers and bristlecone pines are rooted among lichen-covered boulders, polished by wind and snow. The slope drops sharply, eventually disappearing beneath folds of sand. As the sand dunes formed, sand blew in from the San Luis Valley and buried the lower part of the ramp. Now there are dunes that ride up that slope as the dune mass gains 600 feet of elevation at that northern edge.

From the top of the ramp, it is easy going down, as the troughs of dunes that are perched higher on the underlying mountain slope are almost at the height of the crests of the next lower dunes, like a giant staircase cascading down. Going up was a different story, and I needed long breaks. I sat down during my ascent, and my breathing slowed after a minute. After twenty minutes of stillness, I was almost forgotten by the world.

Rabbitbrush seeds blew past me in an eddying breath of air, following the slope. Bird trails wove together in loosely tangled knots between grasses and skeleton weed. Songbird songs opened gently, like winter wildflowers.

A coyote,
on a long, easy path
down massive steps of dune crests and folds,
descending the ramp,
was surprised to find me,
and seemed more annoyed than scared
that I was sitting on his stairs.

The silence of supple curves,
drifting clouds,
speckled rays,
gave way to sudden gale.

Unleashed was Poseyemu,
son of the sun,
rising like his father,
from the brackish waters of Sip'ophe;

and I'm sure that unconfined,
this first of the Tewa
held the form of a red-tailed hawk,
screaming,
untouchable,
spiraling above the dunes.

How ancient and potent a place,
to inspire
our stories of creation.

In Tewa Indian mythology, Poseyemu was the first human to climb out of the underworld. He climbed up a Douglas fir that rose out of the lake Sip'ophe and learned the ways of the middle world from his father, the sun. Modern scholars believe that Sip'ophe could have been the San Luis Lakes, which are just outside of Great Sand Dunes.

Winter Sunrise

Just after sunset, I could see the lakes glowing, covered in ice, from my vantage high on a dune. The heat of day was gone, and my breath had been visible long before the colors had started in the sky. I camped on dry sand just outside of one of the snowfields. By that time, the air was so cold that the stars didn't twinkle.

Lying on my back in the calm night, I traveled through time.

The sky was black,
and the inky dunes had risen on all sides of my lonely tent.
I felt the earth spinning through the hair on the back of my neck,
as I gripped the folds of my sleeping bag with whitening knuckles —
and with a rush I was hurtling through space,
racing the stars.

There is plenty of time.

Later,
Orion,
finally grounded by the weight of his enormous sword,
landed his nightly jeté
on a smooth sand saddle
under the southwestern sky,

before falling off the rim of the world.

Just then an airplane, flashing red and white, cut a swath through the middle of Orion. Thoughts of an ancient world fractured and vanished. The droning sound of engines replaced the silence. But within minutes, a meteor streaked across the sky, erasing the plane, returning me to my mythology.

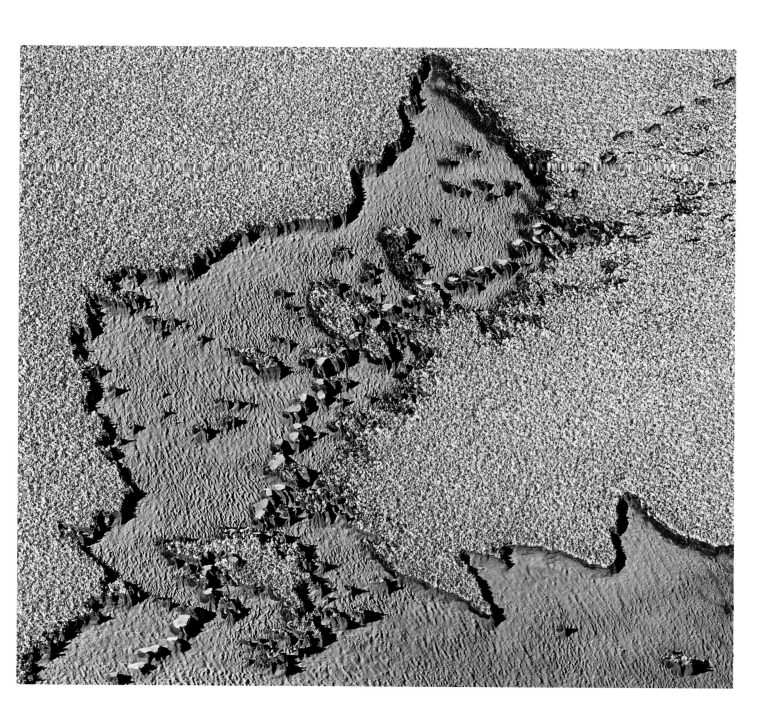

Raised Coyote Tracks through an Eroded Snowfield

Feathered Sand Slides

Winter Dunes and Lifting Clouds

The trek began as a trial. The first day I was walking well before dawn. Cold wind howled and had its way with my balance. I pressed myself against it and against the 115 pounds of my pack and against the unstable sand. The howling got inside my head and took over. Thoughts became rudimentary as I fought my way around the southwest corner of the dune mass and then headed north along the western edge, spending precious energy. My vision funneled straight down, with only enough breadth to plan the next two steps. But the snowstorm was coming; I knew it. I wanted to be in position to see it.

Soon I was winding my way through rabbitbrush, yuccas, and grasses. The ups and downs of the folded, vegetated dunes in the Sand Sheet seemed endless. Huge active dunes loomed to my right, with plumes of wind-borne sand extending thirty feet from the high ridges. The progress was painfully slow, and my face burned from wind and cold. All my muscles screamed. My only reprieve was that the sand on the north-facing slopes of the folds was still frozen and felt good to my feet, hard, in contrast to the loose south-facing slopes that slipped and cascaded underfoot.

Four hours. Six hours. Ten hours. I tried to resist pulling out the watch to meter my progress. The sun set behind a screen of clouds. Finally, after fourteen hours, I found the right spot. Camp was an orphan dune surrounded by Sand Sheet. The clean sand was milky white in the falling light. I set up my tent, still fighting the wind as I dug down a foot to bury the sand stakes, canvas bags that will hold the tent in a seventy-mile-per-hour gale. Inside, the flapping of the wind-fly seemed peaceful compared to the uncompromising howling and whistling that had filled my head throughout the day. Sleep came hard and dreamless. The wind continued to howl.

I awoke in the half dark and stepped out into the soft morning snowstorm. Snow fell in gentle swirling eddies. I stood at the top of the orphan dune as the snow silently collected between its sand ripples. In the broadening sphere of light, I could discern the rabbitbrush, grasses, and distant ghostly dunes, blanketed completely. Thick featureless clouds hid the mountains and sky and flattened the light into a dull sheen. I reveled in the stillness, but even as I did the wind picked up out of nowhere and the snow flew sideways. Shortly, the flakes stopped falling altogether. The buildup on the ground disappeared within minutes, revealing, at my feet, the top half of a kangaroo rat skull with two long orange teeth still embedded in the bone.

Today I would enjoy the wind. First there is a grudging acceptance upon recognizing a day when the wind is not going to stop. Then I quit wanting it to stop and start wanting it to blow harder. I sneaked back to the tent and ate a quick breakfast of Clif Bars and water, packed up my daypack, and returned to the wind.

Wind seems almost sentient at times. It molds the dunes and their inhabitants. Some, like the Great Sand Dunes tiger beetle, need the wind to survive. Biologist Phyllis Pineda Bovin discovered that the endemic tiger beetle can only live in areas of active sand where vegetative cover is less than fifteen percent. Areas with more vegetation don't support the beetles, and vegetation is always creeping up onto the sand. The grasses come first, and the sunflowers. If enough plants take root in a new area, they make way for the rest of the ecosystem by stabilizing the sand. Ten percent vegetative cover will reduce the sand movement by fifty percent. Fifty percent vegetative cover will reduce the sand movement by ninety percent. Drought and wind fight back, creating sandy blowouts, the orphan dunes, maintaining the balance. The tiger beetle owes a debt to the wind.

The storm blew through. The featureless sky took shape and the sun cut keyholes in the clouds, illuminating individual dunes. Two families of coyotes were howling, and I saw the blue streak of a flying mountain bluebird. By one o'clock in the afternoon, the storm was gone, replaced by O'Keeffian clouds and fathomless sky. Everything was in furious motion except for the twisted black branches of dead rabbitbrush, which stood raw and exposed: gnarled knuckles and claws. With the vegetation blurred into abstraction, I could see what was underneath: elk tracks. There were more than I had ever seen or even imagined could exist in one spot. Far from October's great seventy-five-foot-wide swaths of tracks crossing the sand of low dunes in relatively straight thoroughfares, this was an endless labyrinth. There were tracks around every plant. The entire Sand Sheet was a mosaic of them. Because of the reduced sand movement in the Sand Sheet, tracks don't melt into ripples like they do on open sand. The elongated arcs of the dragging toes were gone, but the deep, punctuated divots remained, as did the scat. Elk scat was everywhere.

These were grazing tracks, and they were elegant. The grasses here were not mowed down, but rather browsed selectively. Even in areas where the footprints covered all available space between the plants, three-fourths of the grass stems remained untouched. Not a single plant was visibly trampled. Not a single one.

I walked on. The tracks were truly everywhere. It was not a localized condition. I walked for miles during the course of the day, and it was the same. The Sand Sheet was peppered with tracks and droppings. The tracks were filled with all sorts of riffraff. Tracks concentrated the droppings, which rolled into the divots and stayed at the bottom. On top of the droppings in each track, a latticework of gray downed grasses had collected, crisscrossed with pieces of dried sunflower stalks and all manner of other dried sticks. Each structure was so interlaced it resembled a woven basket. The baskets provided mechanisms to catch the smaller, lighter riffraff like the chaffs of rabbitbrush, tiny spiky yellow pods that open to release the seeds. Finally, caught in the bottom of the baskets were the rabbitbrush seeds—the prizes—like tied fly-fishing flies, now protected from further movement. I watched one of the structures build itself in the gusts. The animals and plants were harmonizing to replant and fertilize the entire rangeland with the help of, and in spite of, the wind.

I watched a tumbleweed bounce across open sand.

At that moment, I realized I was being watched. The wind was just right, so I smelled their musk before I saw them. A group of elk, twelve, had just come to the top of one of the folds 100 yards away. They stood with their heads raised, hyperaware. I looked farther, and a mile northwest I spotted the herd, more than 150 animals. I gingerly set down my pack and assembled a camera with a long lens. The group of twelve held their ground, then turned and walked down into the golden sea and disappeared. I focused on the main herd through my lens, the distortion of heat, wind, and distance softening the image into a Monet.

It was a winter herd: a mixture of females, males, and yearlings. A set of six males trotted in over the sand of an orphaned dune, approaching the main herd. There was a brief standoff, and then they integrated

Wind at Sunset

Layers of Animal Tracks

themselves. Males sparred with each other, locking antlers. At one point there were three sparring matches occurring simultaneously. The mass of animals moved steadily across the tumultuous rolling landscape, disappearing and reappearing in the folds. Three weeks earlier, a big storm had dumped ten inches of snow. As the elk crossed an orphan dune, they munched on the patches of snow preserved in the shadows. I now understood how the elk got their water.

I moved up the ridge a few steps and scared a jackrabbit. In profile, it jumped like a horse going over a barrier, stretched full out. Quick landings were followed by other Superman leaps, all four feet leaving the ground at once. The backs of its ears were white, two alarm beacons, bouncing through the rabbitbrush. The rabbit got to where it thought I couldn't see it, some hundred yards away, and vanished. I had seen exactly where it stopped, but I didn't chase. I did examine the first few tracks. In the first leap, it had covered more than ten feet in the air.

Concentrating on the tracks, I almost missed the next act altogether. Luckily, I looked up just in time. Another herd of elk was running down the wall of sand from the very top of the highest star dunes. There were more than sixty of them. From my vantage more than a mile away, they looked like huge marbles rolling down the dunes. They came down in twos and threes, stopping on the top of each great lip of sand before running down the next slope. One bull trudged slowly all the way to the top of the tallest dune. He stood for a second, outlined against the sky, then he turned on his heels and ran fast down the steep wall, a plume of sand spraying out behind him.

A one-antlered elk led the last group of eight bulls. They paused for a long time on the last ridge, then dropped over the side. Their shadows registered clearly on the sand. Even from so far away, I could see the powerful but delicate strides and imagine their muscles rippling under their skin. Midway down the wall, one bull charged another one from behind. The front bull spun around in full run, locking antlers with his attacker, and they rolled down the dune in a cloud of sand.

I found a place in the midst of the rabbitbrush that was sheltered from the wind and lay down to watch the clouds, and then it was sunset. As the sun dropped away, clouds caught on top of the peaks like cotton candy. The relentless wind had long since found all the cracks in my Gore-Tex shell. My tent was a welcome sight at the end of the day. All of my tracks had been erased. A long wind-shadow extended from the northeast side, and the ripples overlapped in interference patterns—the signature of the southwest wind breaking around the tent. I hadn't drunk enough water during the day. I forced down a quart but still woke in the middle of the night, my back and arms and legs aching from the hiking and dehydration. I downed another full bottle of water and went back to my spinning sleep. The wind stopped sometime during the night.

The morning was frigid and there was no dawn. Another bank of clouds had filled the sky during the night. I ventured out of the tent only to answer nature's call and stretch my sore muscles. As I stood in the somber light, snowflakes started flitting around me like butterflies. I stayed in the tent until ten o'clock and nursed my dehydration hangover. Then I walked out into the grassland without pack or camera. It felt good to be rid of them. Thirty yards upslope I came across tracks of two coyotes that had come through during the night.

Antler and Grasses in Snow Flurries

To the south, heavy clouds with blue-black bottoms hung over the mountains. But overhead, shafts of light shot through everywhere and snow fell halfway to the earth. Birds were singing—not short winter chipping, the essential notes of communication when they flock together looking for seeds, but the lavish songs of spring. Shiny black elk droppings were scattered like forgotten obsidian. A songbird had marked the sand with the imprint of its feathers.

The snow began to fall straight down. A shaft shone through and illuminated me and the hillside. It was the only light on the entire dune field. The rabbitbrush glowed a neon lime green. There was a good wet smell, and every once in a while I got a noseful of strong elk musk and sweet chewed grass. Each snowflake gleamed as it fell. The falling snow got to within a foot of the ground but no farther, sublimating before it touched the sand. I stood comfortably in the warmth of the sun in short sleeves as snowflakes caught in my eyelashes.

From the top of a ridge, I saw the elk again, the same group of eight that had rolled down the dunes the day before. The bull with one antler was still in the lead. I was a good distance away, so they didn't notice that I was there. They were moving and dropped down out of sight into the folds, coming right toward me. I sat down and waited for them. They reappeared on the top of a ridge only a few hundred feet away.

As each one topped the ridge, he gave me a good look. Their muscles rippled. They shook and scratched behind their ears with their rear hooves. One of them backtracked along the top of the ridge, eyeing me the whole time, waiting for me to make my move. If I had so much as sneezed, they would have been gone, running back into the golden folds. But I stayed quiet and they worked their way around me, giving me a 200-foot-wide berth. Finally they looped around and went back to grazing, half a mile away to the west.

Snow fell off and on all day, and I moved freely without my gear. I walked up and down in the Sand Sheet, riding the ridges and waves, dropping into the troughs. The low dunes underlying the Sand Sheet ecosystem were as precise and complex as ripples crossing obliquely on water. There were nodes, long troughs, and rounded hollows. Lost in one of these hollows was a weathered antler, gleaming white against the wet sand and yellow grasses.

Finding the antler was not like finding a skull. This was a more subtle mortality. An animal had aged another year there and passed through, getting on with things. It was quiet. I would come back tomorrow. I sat with the antler the rest of the day.

Rabbitbrush and Snow-covered Dunes #1

Rabbitbrush and Snow-covered Dunes #2

MARCH: AN IMPROBABLE PLACE

When I started down Medano Creek, my breath hung suspended in the predawn air. The cottonwoods were dark line drawings, a tangle of branches and new green buds growing in a narrow corridor. Underneath the trees, raspberry bushes, grasses, and willows were also greening up. Juncos flashed their white tail feathers, flitting through the branches. The flow of the seasonal creek traced the edge of the area, gurgling, swollen with spring runoff. It was a familiar Rocky Mountain scene, except that on the opposite bank of this creek, a 100-foot wall of sand rose steeply, dwarfing the trees, hiding nearly half the sky.

Behind the wall of sand, to the west, lay thirty square miles of active dunes. This imposing eastern wall was continually moving forward but had never reached the trees. It is held back by the narrow creek, which flows in the spring and early summer, defining the eastern and southern edges of the main dune mass. When it flows, the creek carves off towering chunks of sand and washes them downstream, like the ocean working on a glacier. I sat on the creekbank and listened to the water's warbling music, punctuated by the *thunk*-splashes of falling chunks of sand. The edge opposite me calved off, dumping a 15-foot-tall slab into the creek.

It has been said that you can throw a leaf into a Rocky Mountain creek and it will float all the way to the Gulf of Mexico. This is not true for Medano Creek. It is possible to walk the whole course of this paradoxical creek from source to destiny in less than a day.

Water movement in the creek is complex. The creek runs in pulses and waves. For most of its course, Medano's creekbed is composed almost entirely of sand, so the flowing water is full of suspended sand grains. Even at its narrowest, the stream is a braided rope of channels. In areas where the flow through a channel is strong enough, series of underwater divots, called antidunes, form at regularly spaced intervals on the creekbed. Water flows over the antidunes in a procession of standing waves. Both the standing waves and antidunes migrate slowly upstream, amplifying as they go. At a certain point, the waves break into rapids. Gurgling and frothing at their tops, the rapids quickly prove too much for the antidunes. The antidunes vanish in violent swirls of current, reverting to smooth bottom, releasing sand downstream suspended in pulses of water.

The creek was a mosaic of antidune fields. Each field consisted of ten or fifteen antidunes that formed and broke apart in concert, cycling again every twenty seconds. The small pulses of upstream antidune fields sometimes coordinated with one another, forming a large pulse. About once every minute, a two-inch-tall wave came down the creek, wiping out all of the antidune fields, flooding the braided channels. The sound and action of the creek and waves was unnerving. It was as if the mountain above was clearing its throat, about to speak.

I walked downstream. The edges of the creek were clogged with undergrowth on both sides, so I took off my shoes, rolled up my pants, and entered. The water was ice cold, and the sand sucked at my feet. I walked as close to the shore as I could, but the water was still knee-deep. One of the waves came down, raising the water level by a few inches and wetting the bottom of my rolled jeans. I edged around a tight corner, brushing spiderwebs and branches out of my face. There the creek spread out and became shallower. The trees were now

Burned Trees

withdrawn from the shore, so I stepped back onto the bank and dried my legs. I was in a flat, marshy cove full of reeds. Along the edge were the marks of history: three grayed stumps of beaver-downed trees, from when the cove had been a pond.

Bird songs sounded through the trees like tinkling bells. The water burbled. A mile downstream, the creek completed its turn around the southeast corner of the dune mass and headed west. There was now space between the shore of the creek and the dunes to the north, so the creek widened to 200 feet, opening onto the sandy plain. The trees on the south side of the creek had fallen back as well, giving way to low, grass-stabilized dunes. Tangled channels were now separated by sandbars. The water in the channels was dull brown with suspended sand, but the flats between channels were shiny, reflecting the dunes and sky.

Wide shelves of interlaced ice crystals fanned out above the shallowest channels near the shore. The sun rose behind me, and the feathered ice pictures were full of lights. I chose one of the embedded scenes and set up my large-format camera. But just then, a pulse of water flowed under the ice shelf, melting my photograph before my eyes. Then the whole shelf, ten feet wide and eighty feet long, dissolved into the surging water. I looked back upstream. The banks of the creek were cut out of sand. The creek pulsed down in its eerie waves, between dunes and cottonwoods. Above it all, Mount Herard presided, covered in snow. The creek sparkled madly.

Ripples intersected,
crosshatched textures —
liquid light.

Where the creek's channels had shifted, ripple marks were exposed: divots with curved tails. They looked like millions of tadpoles swimming downstream, telling the interweaving stories of former currents. I stepped onto the saturated sand and the ground flexed all around, accepting and distributing my weight. When I released my foot, water flowed back into my footprint and the ground rippled. The water in the sand gleamed in a circle around each step. I was walking on light, squeezing it out from under my boots.

Farther downstream, cottonwoods grew on both sides of the creek, forcing the flow into a narrow riparian corridor again. Willows guarded the banks, roots pointing downstream, urging the creek onward. Small elliptical islands divided the creek. Marshland buffered the edges, with reeds and grasses sticking out like mussed hair. Dried sunflowers from last summer stood six feet tall. I sat on the edge of the creek and savored a juicy orange.

My eyes came to rest on a dead cottonwood marooned in the middle of the sloshing water. Five thick branches radiated out from the main trunk like fingers. I waded out into the creek to look at it. Cottonwoods are able to live in shifting environments such as dunes because they can sprout new roots if they are buried. At one point, this tree had endured a wave of sand. Roots stuck out like hair ten feet up the trunk, showing the previous depth of a dune.

A cool wind brushed my face as I climbed up the bank into a forest of dead cottonwoods, with strips of bark hanging limply from their polished gray trunks. A lightning strike had left one tree just a hollow husk, a blackened chimney. The bark lay in strips over the brush like drying meat. All the limbs had fallen. I could almost see the fire billowing out of the fluted hole at the base of the tree as it burned. Another tree was split in

Medano Creek Sunset Water Detail

half, straight down to the ground. The recoil from that lightning strike was frozen in the twisted halves, which arched away from each other.

I now stood on a high mound that was covered with grass, brush, and trees. On one side was the creek, babbling away below. On the other side lay the murky stagnant water of a wetland with cattails, horsetails, and moss-covered banks encircled by an animal trail. The little wetland was like a jewel, a secret, hidden and protected. Suddenly, an intense gust of wind whipped along the opposite bank of the creek, not 100 feet away, lifting tumbleweeds sixty feet in the air, bending all of the trees. On my side of the creek, the air remained still.

Downstream, the northern bank of the creek tapered down and ended, spilling the creek out onto the sandy plain again. The creek angled away from the dunes, and the flats were now a quarter of a mile wide. Very little grew on the flats. They were covered with memories of wider creeks, left in river rocks evenly spaced over the sand.

Beyond the plain, low dunes were covered with yellow grasses, and beyond that was the dune mass. Medano Creek is the great recycler. All of the sand washed down from the eastern edge is deposited on this open plain south of the dunes and blown back up into the main dune mass, shaping, building up, and elongating the southern edge. Even farther, the white-capped peaks of the Sangre de Cristos formed the last line before the sky took over, arching into clear blue.

I crossed the creek, walking now between the water and the dunes. Pebbles and stones rolled on the sand underneath the water. The mountain was washing down the creek. Joining the pebbles were leaves, bits of bark and wood, pinecones, green pine needles, and an earthworm, passing in the pulses of water. Six ravens floated in just downstream and started strutting their way up the creek, pecking at anything that looked edible. One of the ravens was the same bird I had seen before, missing a feather on its left wing.

The creek dodged and weaved, carving new channels and abandoning old ones. I came across a place where a major channel had just changed and was angling off, forming a pool between two very low dunes on the north side of the creek. For forty minutes it filled up the pool, which conformed to the snaking, rippled shorelines of the two dunes. Then, for unknown reasons, the channel shifted again, rejoining the rest of the creek, cutting off the water supply to the pool. The surface of the water became still, reflecting the dunes beyond. It was one of the most elegant compositions I had ever seen. When I was done photographing, I stripped down, waded out into the middle of the pool, and swam in the snow-cold water. I floated on my back until my body was shivering, then stood in the sun until I was warm again. The water was sinking back into the sand, leaving a dark brown shoreline. In two hours, the pool had completely disappeared.

I wanted to see the end of the creek, so I walked on into the late afternoon, following the sparkling lights on the surface. Sandy foam floated on top of the water and collected on the windward side of the creek. It folded in on itself in long curves and whirls, like the surface of a brain. Water rippled underneath foam, making it pulse.

When I finally arrived, it was nearly sunset. I sat with the water as it trickled and oozed like blood, sinking back into the sand. The polished rocks marking the extent of the creekbed continued west past the end of this year's water, around a bend and out of sight. The water looked metallic in the dying sun. I watched the final fingers of water inch forward over the thirsty plain. It was an improbable place. But just there, I found a water bug, a tiny bronze almond, fighting and kicking its way back up the creek.

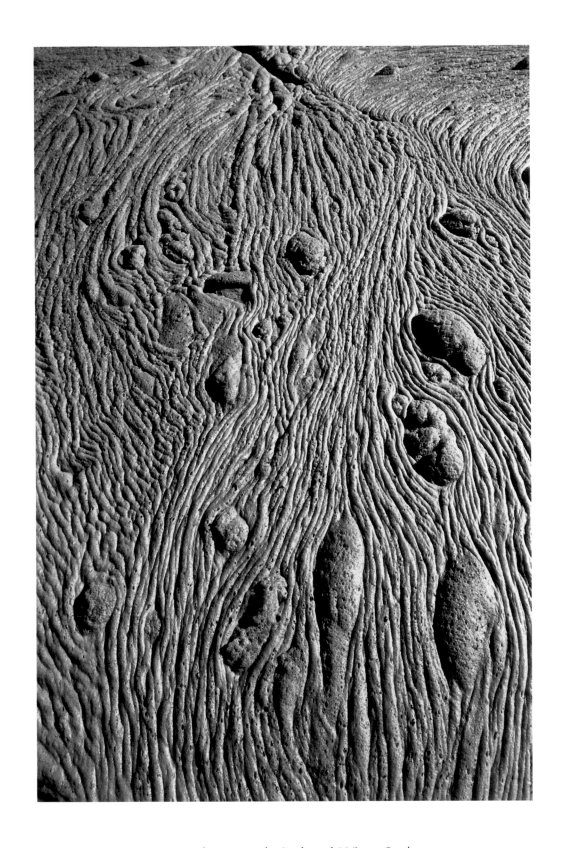

Foam Floating on the Surface of Medano Creek

Former Creekbed

Rippled Shoreline and Reflected Dunes

The End of Medano Creek

Pronghorn and Storm Clouds

APRIL: MAKING WEATHER

Agust of wind surprised me with a mouthful of sand, so I stood up and walked. The winds of April had begun. I hadn't gone fifty yards when I stumbled on a set of tracks. A pronghorn had walked through not long before. Even in the gusty wind, the tracks were deep and sharply defined, toes spread wide. I followed them up an incline and over a low dune, camera ready. As I topped the ridge, the animal was exposed, grazing in an interdunal grassland pocket. He trotted away—not bolting, but making space. He disappeared over a dune, but a minute later came walking back up to the ridge to peer across at me.

A blaze of rust-red and white, he stood on the line between the gray of shifting snow clouds and the gray-brown of shifting sand. I made as few movements as I could manage with the camera. Still, his muscles reflected my presence: Every movement I made sent shivers through his whole body as he reassessed the possible threat. I only took five photographs and then I was out of film. I knew that the process of reloading would scare him, so I sat still. He walked away calmly.

I stayed and watched the wind sweep across the dunes. The clouds blew through, and by sunset, the wind had died. Moonlight filtered down like silver dust, turning the world again into a black-and-white photograph. A deep mist hung around the entire horizon, obscuring the stars. A huge ring, covering a quarter of the sky, surrounded the half-full waxing moon. Orion stood on the outside of the ring, almost overhead. I walked back to my tent slowly and deliberately. It took four hours. Moonlight was sufficient.

The night was warm, so I lay outside my tent as clouds formed across the sky, encroaching on the moon from all sides. The moon held them off as long as it could, but it was a losing battle. I crawled into the tent. Half an hour later, the temperature dropped fifteen degrees and the wind howled. The pinpricks of spring snow on my tent sang me to sleep.

I was camped in a deep dune bowl, and in the morning the sky was a blue circle, cut out of the warm, dry sand. I sat barefoot near my tent and watched insects. A giant sand treader camel cricket was digging a burrow. It shoveled sand under its body with its front two legs, then rocked back and forth on its huge rear legs, pulling the sand farther underneath. Then it leaned forward and kicked the pile away with its rear legs, shooting the sand almost two feet out behind. My seeing the insect midday suggested that its burrow had been disturbed, as the cricket is mainly nocturnal.

Michael Weissmann, a friend and entomologist, told me that male crickets dig a new burrow every night of the breeding season. A male cricket starts digging a burrow in the middle of the night. As he digs, he encourages females to enter but repels other males with his strong kicks. Once inside, the females continue digging, and the male defends the entrance. Before sunrise, the entrance is sealed. By this time, the burrow might measure three feet deep and contain the male and up to four female crickets. The crickets presumably mate during the day, when they are enclosed. At dusk, the crickets abandon the burrow and disperse to forage. In the middle of the night, the male starts digging again, intending to attract another night's harem.

Michael also told me a story about tiny antlike beetles that are endemic to the dunes. The beetles, only a quarter of an inch long, scavenge on dead insects and aphids. Insect carcasses are usually blown easily around the dunes, stopping only in small eddies that move continuously as the wind changes direction. To find these elusive eddies, the beetles climb to the top of a ridge and pull in their legs. They are then picked up by the wind, blown along with the sand and debris, and dropped into the next eddy. There they find food, sometimes flipping over on their backs and grasping a morsel like a sea otter holding onto an abalone shell.

Up the slope, a translucent white caterpillar was working its way across the sand. I moved closer to get a look, but as I did, my shadow fell across the insect, and it reacted immediately. It rolled itself into a wheel, nose to tail, and rolled quickly down the slope, almost down to the tent. After a fifteen-foot tumble, the caterpillar righted itself and at once started inching its way underground to hide. In ten seconds, it had completely disappeared, but the sand still flexed as if it were breathing.

I turned just in time to stop a two-inch-long wolf spider from slipping into my unzipped tent. The spider had two legs over the bottom lip of the door when I brushed it away. On my way into the dunes, I had seen the newly formed silk-lined spider holes all through the Sand Sheet. But this was a dune bowl with forty-foot walls and hardly any vegetation. Dissuaded from the tent, the spider took up residence on one of my boots. It must have been a relief to find a solid wall to block the now gusting wind.

Clouds closed over my blue hole of sky. It was time to walk, so I apologized to the spider as I removed my boot. The arachnid started climbing at once, and by the time I had gotten my boots and pack, it had crested the other side of the dune bowl. I followed it out, and an hour later I was at the edge of the Sand Sheet, looking out over the rabbitbrush, the dune mass behind me.

The raven with the missing feather flew over, circled me twice, and croaked out a comment before passing. I am almost certain it was a croak of recognition. I began picking my way through the rabbitbrush. I had returned specifically to see what had become of February's labyrinth of elk tracks. I wanted to confirm that the seeds caught in the tracks had sprouted.

It didn't take long to find out. The tracks were everywhere, still filled with riffraff interlaced like baskets. Growing up through the baskets were new green shoots of grasses and tiny rabbitbrushes. The elk had done their job. The Sand Sheet was replanted. Then I happened on a bird's nest. It was made of the same gray dried grasses, woven at the base of a rabbitbrush with grasses growing up around. It was obvious that the nest would have been invisible in the summer green.

The nest and the grasses growing up through the tracks were so inextricably tied together that it didn't make sense to think of anything separately. I had to sit down and soak in what I was seeing.

The world seemed to be coalescing in my mind, everything connecting to everything else. There was wind in my hair. I felt on the edge of some essential truth. Elk and grass. I was surrounded by spirits. My mind traced a few more lines of the web. The dunes were contributing to their own weather. The sand collected and released the sun's heat, causing air to rise. The rising air, along with the moisture above it, formed clouds, storms, and wind. Weather, in turn, remolded the dunes, and the cycle continued.

Wolf Spider and Boot

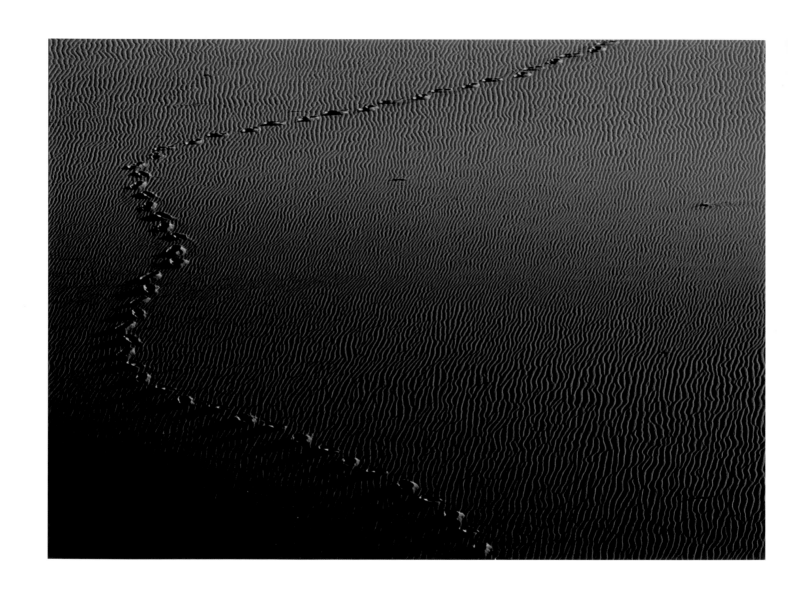

Footprints

I looked back over my shoulder to see my own trail weaving over the dune and then down into the Sand Sheet. Each footprint was shadowed. My footsteps would cause the sand to collect and release heat at a different rate than before I had walked through. By stepping out onto the dunes, I had become a part of them. Each footstep would, in a very minute way, change the wind.

I continued through the rabbitbrush, looking at the progression of tracks. How many other connecting threads surrounded me without my knowledge? In all my time on the dunes, I had never seen mating crickets or wind-borne beetles. How many other wonders had I passed by, or even trampled?

The dunes seemed to flex profoundly all around me. Everything I did had consequence. I was again consumed by a question that had begun to haunt me: How could I love this place without loving it to death? I had learned how to walk more mindfully. I truly watched every single step. But on occasion, I still had caved in kangaroo rat burrows. I had heard roots snap underfoot. And it was not just my presence, but our presence — humanity's in general — that needed consideration. We have such potential to squeeze too hard. I tried to think of every step multiplied by a thousand.

The Sand Sheet gave way to an orphaned dune, and suddenly everything looked familiar. I was back at my campsite from February. This place had been my home for six days. I set my pack down on the clean sand. There was fresh coyote scat where my tent had been. I had an idea. I walked down the dune to the edge of the Sand Sheet and started to search. Again, I found what I was looking for almost immediately. My footprints were still there, preserved among the rabbitbrush. All of the detail in the tracks was gone, but the stride matched perfectly. My eyes brimmed with tears. Each of the tracks was full of riffraff. Growing up through the riffraff were the new green sprouts of spring.

Riffraff and First New Growth

Stairway to the Sky

ACKNOWLEDGMENTS

The story behind this book is one of community. I could write another entire book, and twice as long, detailing the contributions and support that my friends have given to help me along my journey. Just to give an example, my elementary school principal, John Ferree, still comes to all of my openings and sends me cards on my birthday. You have all held me up. I have been truly blessed. My gratitude instructs my life.

Among the people who have given me inspiration, encouragement, advice, financial support, career direction, jobs, companionship, longstanding friendship, and love are the following: Steve Jones and Nancy Dawson; William Neill; Perry Conway and Susanna Block; Jim Balog; Rich Clarkson; Donald and Rosalee Culver; John Martin and Gina Martin-Smith; Bob and Maureen Hoffert; Rit and Linda Carbone; Ron and Susan Crowell; Wayne and Chris Itano; Gary Zeff and Boulder Open Studios; David Schonauer of *American Photo* magazine; Sadhna, Tara, and Ravi Neill; Peter Mortimer; Jared Carbone and Kimberly Gilbert; Andrew Valdez, Phyllis Pineda Bovin, Carol Sperling, Kris Illenberger, Patrick Myers, Fred Bunch, and the rest of the Great Sand Dunes staff; Mark Burget and Audrey Wolk of The Nature Conservancy; Michael Weissmann; Jeanne DeNoyer; Heidi Geisz; Leslie Dawe; Mark Lellouch; Wendy Wempe; Justin Weihs; Taran Reese; Brendan Turrill; Jeremy Kassis; Erik Burns; Cameron Weise; Elizabeth Cope; Brian Hugli; Rich and Susan Seiling, Jeff Grandy, and Terrance Reimer of West Coast Imaging; John Botkin of Photocraft Labs; Sunnie and Steve Nissen of Broomfield Creative Framing; Lidwina Clements; Hilton and Ann Osborne; Brian Muldoon and Susan Hall; Chris Brown and Elizabeth Black; Claudia Welsh, Michael Frye, and Glenn Crosby of The Ansel Adams Gallery; Karen Weihs of the White Moon Gallery; Nikki, Lonnie, and Lou LaMontagne; Niles Utlaut; Jay Maisel; Donna Gartenmann of the Boulder Arts Commission; Emilie Upczak of BMoCA; Chris Johns and Bill Allen of *National Geographic* magazine; and David Ashcraft of the David Ashcraft Gallery. A special thanks goes to Marilee Langner, who accompanied me to see the shooting stars. A special thanks also goes to John Fielder, Linda Doyle, Mark Mulvany, Jenna Browning, Craig Keyzer, Martha Gray, and the rest of Westcliffe Publishers. Finally, without the support and love of my sister, Molly, and my parents, Emily and Steve, none of this would have been possible.

International Standard Book Number: 1-56579-514-8

Text and photography copyright: John B. Weller, 2004. All rights reserved.

Editor: Jenna Samelson Browning
Designer: Mark Mulvany
Production Manager: Craig Keyzer

Published by:
Westcliffe Publishers, Inc.
P.O. Box 1261
Englewood, CO 80150

Printed in China by: C & C Offset Printing, Ltd.

Library of Congress Cataloging-in-Publication Data:
Weller, John B., 1974-
  Great Sand Dunes National Park : between light and shadow / photography and text by John B. Weller.
    p. cm.
  ISBN 1-56579-514-8
  1. Great Sand Dunes National Park (Colo.)--Pictorial works. 2. Landscape--Colorado--Great Sand Dunes National Park--Pictorial works. 3. Natural history--Colorado--Great Sand Dunes National Park--Pictorial works. 4. Great Sand Dunes National Park (Colo.)--Description and travel. 5. Weller, John B., 1974---Travel--Colorado--Great Sand Dunes National Park. I. Title.
F782.G78W45 2004
917.88'49--dc22   2004052620